Subtle Sound

SUBTLE SOUND

The Zen Teachings of *Maurine Stuart*

Edited with an introduction by
ROKO SHERRY CHAYAT

Foreword by
EDWARD ESPE BROWN

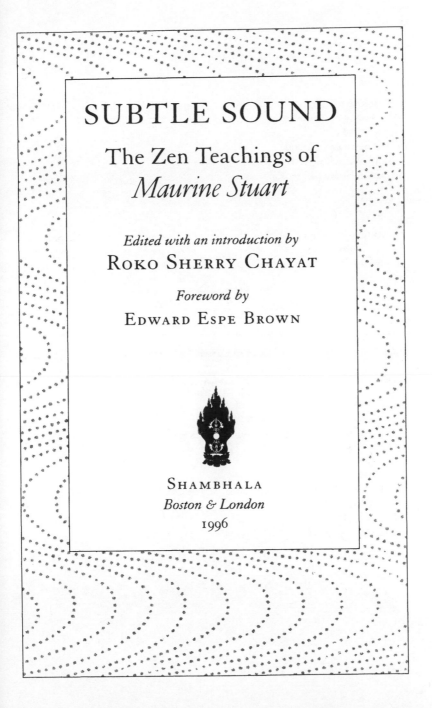

SHAMBHALA
Boston & London
1996

SHAMBHALA PUBLICATIONS, INC.
Horticultural Hall
300 Massachusetts Avenue
Boston, Massachusetts 02115
www.shambhala.com

© 1996 by Sherry Chayat

Printed in the United States of America

Distributed in the United States by Random House, Inc.,
and in Canada by Random House of Canada Ltd

LIBRARY OF CONGRESS CATALOGING-IN-PUBLICATION DATA

Stuart, Maurine.
    Subtle sound: the Zen teachings of Maurine Stuart/edited with an
    introduction by Roko Sherry Chayat; foreword by Edward Espe Brown.
    —1st ed.
        p.   cm.
    ISBN 1-57062-094-6 (alk. paper)
    1. Spiritual life—Zen Buddhism.   2. Zen Buddhism—Doctrines.
    I. Chayat, Sherry.   II. Title.
BQ9288.S78   1996   96-16430
294.3'4—dc20   CIP
BVG 01

· · ·

THIS BOOK IS DEDICATED TO
MAURINE'S STUDENTS EVERYWHERE.

Let true Dharma continue!

· · · · ·

Contents

Credits

For her references to koans and the teachings of early Zen masters, Maurine Stuart Roshi used as principal sources *Two Zen Classics: Mumonkan and Hekiganroku*, translated by Katsuki Sekida (New York: Weatherhill, 1977), and *The Record of Lin-chi*, translated by Ruth F. Sasaki (Kyoto: Institute for Zen Studies, 1975). She used the *Sutra Book* published by The Zen Studies Society, New York, for its compilation of excerpts from sutras and texts.

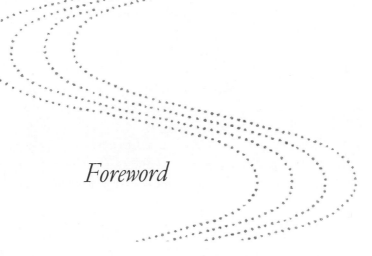

Foreword

R EADING OVER these talks by my friend and teacher Maurine Stuart Roshi, I am struck by a simple fact. There are no secrets here. Nothing is revealed. If you are seeking to get an insight or saying that does something for you, you will find nothing in these talks. What is found will be in you yourself, your own treasure. As Dogen Zenji said about a good teacher, "Even if the wood is bent, placed in skilled hands its splendid merits immediately appear." Maurine wants you to know the splendid merits that are yours.

This is Maurine's great gift, her genius, her realization—to give you your independence rather than taking it away. This is far more difficult than it sounds. The temptation to which many teachers succumb is to offer insights and understandings, brilliant and articulate words that often leave the student feeling dumb and unworthy, dependent on the teacher for the next spiritual fix, for the right understanding. Maurine is careful to let you stand on your own: "We are working together, sitting together, helping each other, but not in a way that we become dependent on each other's help. . . . We have a clean, clear friendship, without expectations and without demands." (From

"The Illusion of 'I' ") Maurine was not someone who needed to impress or dazzle anybody with her understanding. She was simply intent on awakening others to what was already theirs.

My teacher Shunryu Suzuki Roshi would say at times, "The important point is to own your own body and mind," and, "When you are you, Zen is Zen." Maurine was someone who lived this teaching. She was clear and true at honoring who she was, what she felt, and handling it. She didn't need to prove how "Zen" she was. She wasn't about to cover up who she was or adopt pretense. Straightforward and forthright, Maurine was also a deeply passionate person, yet she wasn't spendthrifty with emotion.

I first met Maurine in the summer of 1984, when I had the opportunity to drive her and her husband over the fourteen-mile dirt road into Tassajara Zen Mountain Center in the Santa Lucia Mountains in California. While Maurine and I conversed in the front seats, her husband sat white-lipped behind us silently regarding the steep drop-offs. After a while my daughter, who was twelve, finally said to him, "You don't talk much, do you?" It was a light moment, and Maurine appreciated the innocent subtlety of my daughter overlooking the obvious trepidation while remarking on the lack of conversation in the back seat.

This was also when I first heard Maurine speak, and I must confess to being startled by the sheer power of her voice. While so many speakers drone on, or their voices are so small as to imply that what they have to say is not really that important, Maurine's voice was so incredibly full-bodied that I wondered where it was coming from and whether that voice could really be hers. Unfortunately readers will not be able to hear the resonance and vibrancy, the spirited and dramatic quality of her words. *Crescendo* and *decrescendo, pianissimo* and *fortissimo,* her being was an instrument that played inside her listeners, bringing something hidden alive.

After that meeting at Tassajara, I would visit Maurine at the

Cambridge Buddhist Association on Sparks Street. The atmosphere was austere, yet sweet and focused, a wonderful contrast to the Nityananda Institute nearby, where I would visit friends. Their meditation hall was lively and colorful with lifesize statues and large paintings of various teachers in their lineage. I'd think, "How wonderful." By comparison, Sparks Street was bare, yet the single scroll or small statue held tremendous power, a few simple things honored and cared for, and I would know, "I'm home."

Maurine did not fool around, and she was nobody's fool. She took people seriously, and when she said you could do it, you could believe her, even if it was difficult. "How willing are you to really know who you are? Many of us are afraid to do that. We just take the soft, pallid approach: 'Oh, this makes me feel good. Ah yes, I feel better now.' Sometimes I want to say, 'I'm sorry about that.' I wish you felt something so deeply that then, eventually, you'd have true peace of mind. Then, no matter what comes, it won't knock you about." (From "Taking It Home")

This is not someone who conveys a subtle grasp of the ineffable, but your steadfast friend reminding you of simple truths: "One act, one place," and, "While you are doing (zazen), please don't judge it. Or I should rather say, when it is doing you, don't judge it. 'My zazen is going well.' Nonsense." (From "Taking It Home")

Maurine was a steadfast friend and spiritual companion to many people, and now readers who did not have the good fortune to meet her in person will have the chance to do so through these talks. While it is rather nonsensical to attempt to take the measure of a person or a Zen teacher who is essentially beyond measure, I would say, as Paul Reps used to say about someone he respected, "At least she had her head on straight." Meeting her through these talks will certainly encourage readers to have their heads on straight as well.

I would like to honor Maurine Stuart Roshi with one of the

statements my teacher Suzuki Roshi made that I found deeply penetrating: "Don't move. Just die. Moment after moment. This is your last moment, so nothing can save you now. Not even enlightenment will help you now, because this is your last moment. So be true to yourself and express yourself fully."

I don't claim to have the eye of a master, but from where I sit Maurine embodied this spirit fully, right to the end. Without moving she expressed herself fully. Without looking around for help she was settled in the present moment manifesting the virtue of Zen vitality. Her words ceaselessly encourage us to do the same: "It is your life's work to wake up to the fact that you are enlightened from the beginning. So for me to do anything is redundant, superfluous, and downright intrusive." (From "Taking It Home")

Thank you, Maurine, for your resolute spirit, your wondrous practice, and your resonant words. May we all realize this complete and perfect Awakening.

—Edward Espe Brown

Acknowledgments

MANY PEOPLE WERE INSTRUMENTAL in bringing this book about. I am particularly grateful to Sheila LaFarge, who organized the lengthy and complicated process of gathering and duplicating the tapes of Maurine's teisho, as well as to Billy Meegan and Amie Diller for their time-consuming efforts in this regard.

For their diligent work in transcribing many of these tapes, my gratitude extends to Carol Costa and to several students of the Zen Center of Syracuse, especially to Jennifer Waters, who assumed the lion's share of this task; and to Howard Blair, Terrance Keenan, Scott Rosecrans, Catherine Cooney, Damir Jamsek, Janis Alden-Jones, and Gail Palmer.

My deep appreciation goes to my Dharma brother Peter Matthiessen and my editor, Emily Hilburn Sell, for their warm encouragement regarding this project.

I am profoundly grateful for the loving support of my husband, Andy Hassinger, and my son, Jesse Hassinger, each of whom had his own very special relationship with Maurine.

No words can express my gratitude to my teachers: Eido Shimano Roshi, Soen Nakagawa Roshi, and Maurine Stuart Roshi.

Introduction

MYOON MAURINE STUART ROSHI taught by being. She
often paraphrased Emerson: "Who you are speaks so
loudly I can't hear a word you're saying."[1] Unconditionally, un-
hesitatingly, unreservedly, she gave herself away—as a pianist,
as a Zen practitioner, as a Zen teacher. Although widely read,
she was not a scholar, but rather considered each of the great
teachers of old her intimate friend. Her lively and penetrating
mind relished good conversation, but she was quick to extricate
herself from either small talk or pontification. Wide-ranging in
her interests, she delighted in the wonders of nature and of
human endeavors in music, movies, art, dance, literature, and
food. She loved to drive, and she drove fast, with a single-
minded intensity that brooked no interference no matter what
the elements, what the traffic. She was a true friend, relishing
the quiet rapport of a shared cup of tea or a walk, yet no moment was insignificant; teaching was everywhere.

She had a way of making the person she was with feel special,
as if no one else could ever intrude. A hug from Maurine was
like none other: powerful, energizing. The enveloping warmth
of spirit she conveyed was as bracing as it was tender. Her mag-

netism drew students from far and wide, a few of whom, due to their own unresolved conflicts and unhealed wounds, misunderstood her attentiveness when she was with them and came away with certain self-aggrandizing notions. Rather than disabusing them outright, her method was gently to point a student in the direction of self-correcting insight. Likewise, her compassion for those in pain often overcame her impatience with clinging, dependence, and sentimentality.

I was fortunate to know Maurine over a period of twenty years, during which she evolved from a Zen student of remarkable dedication and determination to a Zen teacher of extraordinary insight and ability. After moving from New York City to Boston in 1970, she began sitting alone, but it didn't take long for others to find her. Continuing her own training *sesshin* after sesshin (an intensive meditation retreat), gradually she accepted the yoke of teacher. In the early 1980s, she began giving *teisho* (formal presentations of the Dharma) at the Cambridge Buddhist Association and at Zen centers throughout the country. After listening to her talks with mounting admiration, I suggested to her that they be compiled into a book. Typically modest in her response, she said, "If you think there is something that might be helpful in any of them, please do so." Coincidentally, she had recently had a visit from our mutual friend Peter Matthiessen and his editor at Shambhala Publications, Emily Hilburn Sell, who also had expressed interest in a book of Maurine's Dharma talks. Maurine suggested I get in touch with Mrs. Sell, which I did, and so this project began. Arrangements were made for me to receive tapes of the Dharma talks she had delivered not only at the Cambridge Buddhist Association, but at Green Gulch Farm, Providence Zen Center, and several other practice centers, in addition to the tapes I had made of her talks at the Zen Center of Syracuse.

Maurine's voice, as all who knew her are keenly aware, was a marvelous Dharma vehicle, and words on a page cannot recreate that experience. Still, her ability to articulate subtle and profound insights in direct and vivid ways can be readily appreciated through the written word. Throughout this project, I have sought to retain Maurine's calm, measured, yet emphatic way of speaking, while editing for clarity and to avoid repetition. In a few cases, where thematic correspondences have warranted it, segments of two or more talks have been woven together.

Since Maurine's teachers were Japanese, she tended to use Japanese names for such Chinese masters as Lin-chi (Rinzai) and Chao-chou (Joshu), with the exception of Hui-neng. I have followed her usage, and have provided the Chinese names in the glossary. Although each of her talks typically began with the reading of a *koan* or a quotation from the ancient masters, for the purposes of this book I have concentrated on Maurine's own words, which refer back to the quoted material the way jazz improvisations do to a melody. Maurine herself continually stressed that these ancient texts cannot be understood historically, but that they must be grasped in their present-tense relevance to our lives.

Despite her respect for the traditional forms of Zen, a respect natural to one whose entire life was engaged in the demanding discipline of music, Maurine's teaching, like her life, was never circumscribed by ritual or convention. The circumstances of daily life provide us with endless numbers of inconceivably subtle koan; Maurine was always right there, sharply attentive to every possibility. In her formal presentations and encounters—in her teisho and *dokusan* (private encounters between teacher and student)—she observed the traditional rituals, but within those conventions, she emphasized a direct, intimate, personal relationship. She never spoke about Buddhist teachings or Zen practice as something outside ourselves. The pronoun "we" pervades each teisho, reminding us that each koan is very much our own story. These dialogues may have taken place in some ancient time and culture, but through Maurine's reenactment, we experience them ourselves. Maurine lived Rinzai, lived

Joshu; and they live through her words, inspiring us as they did their own students.

It has been a great privilege to have spent the years since Maurine's death listening to these tapes over and over and working on their presentation, consulting her now and then in my *zazen*, looking at her looking at me from the photograph on my altar. "Heart-mind to heart-mind" were her last words to me as she touched her forehead to mine after Rohatsu sesshin, December 1989.

My first encounter with Maurine was at a weekend sesshin at the Zen Studies Society's New York Zendo Shobo-ji. It was in the early part of 1970, soon after I had become a member. During sesshin, we women slept on the carpeted floor of the second-floor library. We would stow our sleeping bags and other belongings in a walk-in closet, where we also kept our meditation robes. That first morning, having been thrust by the shrill tones of the *shinrei* (wake-up bell) into a mixture of grogginess and panic, I rolled up my sleeping bag, got in line to use the bathroom, then scurried into the closet to change into my robe. Certain I couldn't last through pre-dawn morning service and zazen without something to eat, I pulled a bag of dried fruit from my coat pocket, and sat down among the sleeping bags underneath the coatrack.

An imposing woman with beautiful red hair came in as I was furtively nibbling away. Caught, I held out the bag to her. Picking out one apricot with exquisite grace, she smiled, and suddenly all my ill-defined, stomach-clenching sesshin fears melted away. After sesshin ended, I had a chance to speak with her, and was struck again by her warmth, dignity, and humor.

Later that year, Maurine had to leave New York City. Her husband, Oscar (Ozzie) Freedgood, had relocated his game and toy manufacturing business to Boston; he, Maurine, and their three school-age children, Barbara, Elaine, and Marc, moved into a large suburban house in Chestnut Hill. Maurine was devastated by the change from the exciting milieu of Upper West

Side Manhattan to what she felt was a cultural wasteland, made more unbearable by a neighbor who took delight in pointing out her every deviation from the social norm. She was terribly homesick for New York City, which she loved not only because of its cultural vitality, an important consideration for a gifted concert pianist, but because it had become her spiritual home.

Music and meditation had, in fact, been intertwined strands at the core of her being since early childhood—long before she ever knew anything about Zen.

Maurine was born on March 3, 1922. The most influential figure in her early childhood was her maternal grandfather, Sam Haight, who worked a 640-acre farm in Saskatchewan, Canada, with loving and meticulous care. The son of a wrathful preacher, he had little use for what he considered the platitudes and hypocrisy of organized religion. His own beliefs tended toward an idiosyncratic blend of pacifism and socialism, but he eschewed any and all platforms. What particularly struck Maurine was the way he treated every being, sentient and insentient alike, with respect and appreciation.

Her immediate family lived in the small town of Keeler, where her father owned a bank and her mother ran a proper household and made sure that her three children were exposed to the important cultural refinements. Fortunately for Maurine, these included music lessons. She took to the piano avidly, sensing its grandeur, its potential for taking her beyond the petty-minded atmosphere of small-town preoccupations. In addition to music, she was nourished by her frequent visits to her grandparents' farm, with its sod-roofed house, and by her solitary forays into the prairie, where she would sit absolutely still for hours at a time, infused with a feeling of intimacy with every blade of grass, every breeze.

At the age of eleven, her life changed radically. Sponsored by friends of the family who were impressed with her talent and intelligence, Maurine was sent to Riverbend School, a boarding school in Winnepeg, Manitoba. It was a period of aching loneliness; she felt out of place and terribly homesick. Once again, music provided solace, and the chance to express emotions that were even more rigidly suppressed there than they had been at home. She stuck it out, and did well in all her academic subjects except religion (which she failed because of her refusal to swallow Biblical scripture unquestioningly). She began giving piano lessons at the age of twelve, and continued doing so for the rest of her life. After graduating, Maurine stayed on at Riverbend to teach music. Continuing her own studies at the music department of the University of Manitoba, she began performing in concerts throughout the western United States and Canada. She was enthusiastically received, and among her many awards was one from the French government that enabled her to study with Robert and Gaby Casadesus and Nadia Boulanger at the American Conservatory in Fontainebleau, as well as with Alfred Cortot, considered one of the greatest piano theorists of the century. Cortot was so impressed with Maurine that he gave her free lessons. Both Boulanger and Cortot were inspiring and demanding in ways that went beyond the discipline of music. Everything they did seemed embued with a profound level of understanding, and their influence on her, like Sam Haight's, was deep and life-long.

Maurine loved France, and drank deeply of all the great art, music, literature, and cafe life that was Paris in 1949. It was while abroad that she came upon the book that would point her toward the other strand of her life's work: *The Story of Oriental Philosophy,* by L. Adams Beck. A reference to meditation in the last chapter, "The Teachings of Zen," was tucked away and, although not further investigated for some fifteen years, never forgotten. "I knew right away that this was it," she told me. "But when I returned to the United States, there didn't seem to be any process through which I could learn more about Zen."

She established herself in New York City, married Ozzie, and with characteristic vigor, managed to continue performing professionally while raising their children. "One day," she said,

"I was doing some housework. I turned on the television, and there was a small man with bushy eyebrows, talking about Zen! It was Dr. D. T. Suzuki, of course."

Part of her routine during those early years was to walk her children to and from school. One morning, something prompted her to take a different route home. Walking along West End Avenue, she saw a sign on a brownstone on the corner of West Eighty-first Street. It read, "Zen Studies Society." She rang the bell; a young monk, Tai-san (as Eido Tai Shimano Roshi was then known), came to the door. "I asked if I could come in to learn about Zen. He stuck a piece of paper with the sitting schedule in my hand and closed the door." A few days went by; then, while strolling in Riverside Park, she came upon a small, thin figure with large, translucent ears and a shaved head, wearing the black robes of a Zen monk—and sneakers. It was, she found out later, Hakuun Yasutani Roshi. "I looked at him, he looked at me, and we moved on." Soon afterward, she returned to the Zen Studies Society, attending two beginners' workshops part-time. "The children were sick, so I couldn't stay the whole time for either of them," she recalled. It was a foretaste of the difficult dilemmas she would soon face, pulled in one direction by family concerns, in another by her music, and in yet another by the imperatives of strenuous Zen practice.

The next time she went to the *zendo,* she saw a sign-up sheet for a week-long sesshin with Yasutani Roshi to be held at Pumpkin Hollow, the Theosophical Society's retreat center in Clarenville, New York. "I put my name down immediately," she said. "One of the senior students, Sylvan Busch, called me up later and asked me if I knew what a sesshin was. He wanted to know if I could get up early in the morning. I told him I always did that anyway. He asked if I could sit still. 'Oh, yes,' I said. 'Well, then, I guess you can go.'"

The day came. Maurine boarded the train to Clarenville with Ruth Lilienthal, Lillian Friedman, and several other Zen students, and their excitement was evident, for the conductor came over and asked them where they were off to. "We're going to a place in the mountains," someone explained. "Will there be entertainment? A floor show?" he asked. Not quite sure of what she meant, Maurine found herself saying, "Oh, yes, the floor show goes on all day."

When they arrived, the place seemed rather strange; there was a main house filled with furniture, and there were several small cottages in the woods. The first order of business was to move all the furniture out of the living room and pile it in another room; then they covered the windows with white sheets. Newcomers like Maurine were asked to meet with Yasutani Roshi in a special ceremony to formalize the student-teacher bond; each presented him with ten dollars in incense money. She remembered being asked, "Are you here to do *bompo* Zen, or are you here to become enlightened?" Maurine didn't know what they were talking about, but must have given the right answer, for then they were ushered into sesshin.

"The flies were terrible. Just constant. No one told me anything about the many rituals, the bowing; at the end of the day, I decided it was just impossible to go on. I had made a mistake. I had had it with this Zen stuff."

"This Zen stuff" also included barked commands and an atmosphere of general hysteria. Students were urged toward *kensho* (the realization of one's Buddha-nature) through shouting, exhorting, and the liberal use of the *keisaku* ("encouragement stick"). To make matters worse, the pain from an old skiing accident was making the fourteen or so hours of sitting in the cross-legged posture physically unbearable. She called Ozzie and told him she was ready to go home. Reminding her of how much she had wanted to go, he encouraged her to try it for one more day. "I stuck it out, through nights of hideous laughter on the part of one of the students, and through days of terrible pain, and things did get better." One day, in dokusan, hearing of her physical plight, Yasutani Roshi (through Tai-san as interpreter) told her just to sit any way she could, and she eventually found a posture—straddling two cushions—that she could maintain.

"By the fifth day, that was that," she recalled. "I was hooked. I knew I would go to every single sesshin from then on." And she had developed a real appreciation for Yasutani Roshi, despite his exhortatory methods. "The most resistant student finally knew that he was there for them," she told Helen Tworkov in an interview many years later, "present with wholehearted effort to wake them up, that the boundless vow to 'save all beings' was compressed into this small, frail body."[2]

Yasutani Roshi was the Dharma heir of Sogaku Harada Roshi. Each had trained in both Soto and Rinzai monasteries, and it was Harada Roshi's emphasis on strenuous practice and kensho that shaped Yasutani Roshi's teaching style. Hakuun Yasutani was born into a very poor family, and his mother was determined that he become a priest. She left him at a temple when he was only four years old; he refused to eat or talk, and finally the monks had to ask his mother to take him back. A year later, he agreed to go off to a small Rinzai temple, Terakoya, which was a school as well; the head priest was called "teacher" by the villagers. "The education that priest gave me was very strict, but very affectionate," he recalled in his 1969 book *Zen and Life*.[3]

Yasutani Roshi's first trip to the United States was in the summer of 1962, for sesshin in Honolulu and Los Angeles, followed by visits every year until 1969, with the exception of 1964. During each of these, his attendant monk was Eido Tai Shimano, and sesshin were held in New York, Pennsylvania, California, and Hawaii. Tai-san was a student of Soen Nakagawa Roshi, the abbot of Ryutaku-ji. Soen Roshi was a brilliant graduate of Tokyo Imperial University. As a young man, he was admired for the breadth of his scholarship in both Eastern and Western subjects, and for his remarkable poetry. Rather than reap the worldly rewards promised by a degree from such a prestigious university, he followed his dream and became a monk. He was ordained by Keigaku Katsube Roshi, who led a Zen group in Tokyo, and it was while he was his attendant monk that he first met Yasutani Roshi, who at the time held the same position with Sogaku Harada Roshi, also in Tokyo. One day, Monk Soen was sent to borrow a keisaku from a nearby Zen group, Hakusan Dojo, and stayed to listen to a teisho by Gempo Yamamoto Roshi, abbot of Ryutaku-ji. It was the beginning of a profound relationship. In 1950 Soen Nakagawa became his Dharma heir and abbot of Ryutaku-ji.

In 1955, Tai-san, who had trained at Empuku-ji and Heirin-ji before becoming Soen Roshi's disciple, met Nyogen Senzaki, one of the most important pioneers of Zen in America, who had come back to Japan for his first and, as it turned out, his last visit. In 1957, Soen Roshi asked Tai-san to move to America to become Senzaki's attendant. A correspondence between the elderly teacher and the young monk began. But on May 7, 1958, a telephone call came; Nyogen Senzaki had died. Two years later, Soen Roshi sent Tai-san to assist a small Zen group in Hawaii. While on a brief visit back to Japan, he accompanied Soen Roshi on a visit to Yasutani Roshi, who was living in the suburbs of Tokyo. A series of five-day sesshin had been set up with a group of American students, most of whom had studied in Japan with either Soen Roshi or Yasutani Roshi. Soen Roshi asked Yasutani Roshi to join him on this sesshin tour of 1962; Tai-san would go along as attendant monk. Just before their departure, however, Soen Roshi's beloved mother took ill, and he was unable to go. She died later that year.

Yasutani Roshi and Tai-san left for America. At Soen Roshi's request, Tai-san continued his koan study with Yasutani Roshi. The tour was a great success, and the following year, Yasutani Roshi asked Tai-san to accompany him on a trip around the world. At the end of 1964, Eido Tai Shimano left Hawaii for good, arriving in New York City on New Year's Eve. In the beginning of 1965, he conducted zazen at the Buddhist Academy on Riverside Drive, then at a small sublet apartment; later that year, he took a lease on a larger space on the corner of West Eighty-first Street and West End Avenue, and Yasutani Roshi joined him there until January 1966, when he returned to Japan. As the number of students grew, Tai-san felt the need for some organizational support, and he consulted his friend, Dr. Bernard Phillips, who was vice president of the Zen Studies Society. The society had been founded in 1956 by Cornelius Crane "to introduce the cultural, educational, and spiritual aspects of Zen Buddhism to the West," but after Mr. Crane's death in 1962, had become inactive. Learning of Tai-san's Dharma work, the board asked him to become a member. With his sense of purpose, and the enthusiasm of the fledgling *Sangha,* the not-for-profit organization was revitalized to support the activities of the newly named New York Zendo.

In 1968, through the generosity of a couple who wished to remain anonymous, the Zen Studies Society was able to purchase a home of its own, a former carriage house at 223 East Sixty-seventh Street. Both Yasutani Roshi and Soen Roshi, who had not been to America in several years, came that summer. First, Tai-san joined them for sesshin in Los Angeles, where Senzaki's students were continuing their practice; then two sesshin were held near New York City. On September 15, 1968, more than two hundred people gathered for the dedication and official opening of the New York Zendo Shobo-ji (Temple of True Dharma). Among them, of course, was Maurine, who had been sitting with Tai-san and, true to her word, had been participating in nearly every sesshin in the New York area since her first one in 1965. She had also been studying with Charlotte Selver, the founder of the sensory awareness movement in the United States.

From the moment Maurine first encountered Soen Roshi at an evening sitting at the New York Zendo that summer of 1968, she felt a remarkable connection, one she likened to "an open channel." She found Soen Roshi's teaching style quite different from that of Yasutani Roshi. Soen Roshi preferred to allow students to ripen at their own rate. His zazen was inspiring in its palpable profundity—he often sat through *kinhin* after kinhin (the walking meditation that serves as a bridge between zazen periods)—and his teisho and dokusan meetings were filled with spontaneity, humor, loving-kindness, and poetry. He was passionately fond of theater, music, and literature, and was famous in Japan for his haiku. Goethe and Beethoven were among his favorite Western artists, and at the conclusion of sesshin that summer, the participants were treated to the "Ode to Joy" from Beethoven's *Ninth Symphony.*

After the opening of the new zendo, Soen Roshi performed a *jukai* (precepts) ceremony for those students who had been sitting for several years. He gave Maurine a *rakusu* (the abbreviated, less formal version of the *kesa,* the pieced-together robe worn by Buddhist monks since ancient times) and the name MyoOn, "Subtle Sound." From that point on, Soen Roshi visited nearly every year, particularly since Yasutani Roshi, increasingly frail, was unable to return after 1969. On March 28, 1973, at the age of eighty-eight, Hakuun "White Cloud" Yasutani passed away while sitting in zazen.

Practice at the New York Zendo was vibrant, with a solid core of long-time students who, like Maurine, had begun sitting at the West Eighty-first Street apartment and who were enthusiastically participating in sesshin with Soen Roshi and Eido-Shi, as Tai-san was now called, first at the Montfort House of Renewal, a Catholic retreat center in Litchfield, Connecticut, run by the Daughters of Wisdom, and later on, at Dai Bosatsu Zendo, a monastery the Zen Studies Society established on the banks of Beecher Lake, high in the Catskill Mountains. The 1,400-acre wilderness tract was purchased in 1971; the first sesshin was held that very year, in the existing lodge on the property. The following year, Soen Roshi returned to lead summer sesshin at Litchfield and at Beecher Lake, and on September 13, he and Eido-Shi performed a "mountain opening" ceremony in which they asked forgiveness of the spirits of the mountain, lake, and field for the "destruction and pollution of all rocks, trees, grasses, and mosses" and "permission to establish a Zen monastery on this very site."

Two days later, in a ceremony at the New York Zendo on its fourth anniversary, Soen Roshi transmitted his Dharma to Eido Tai Shimano and installed him as abbot. Eido Roshi was given the name Mui Shitsu ("True Man Without Rank") as Soen Roshi's Dharma heir. Work continued at the mountain center, with a small group of students living and practicing together year-round in the lodge during the construction of the new monastery, which was completed by the end of 1975. The formal opening of International Dai Bosatsu Zendo was held July 4, 1976, the bicentennial of the United States. It was attended by roshis, monks, nuns, lay practitioners, and Buddhist dignitaries from all over the world.

In 1965, the year Eido Tai Shimano began his Dharma work in New York City and the year Maurine first came upon the Zen Studies Society, I was graduated from Vassar College and moved to New York City. Although no courses in Buddhism had been offered at Vassar, I had read whatever I could find on Zen. I had been sitting since childhood, with no knowledge that there was something called Zen until coming upon a brief description of it in an eighth-grade textbook on world culture. Some day, I thought, I would go to Japan to find a teacher and begin formal training. In 1967 Lou Nordstrom and I decided to get married in a Zen ceremony. Looking in the telephone book under Z, we discovered that the Zen Studies Society was just a few blocks away. Walking down West End Avenue, we came to the address and rang the bell. A young monk answered; it was Eido Tai Shimano. When he heard our request, he invited us in and, after probing our sincerity, agreed to perform the ceremony. On September 2, surrounded by a small group of friends, we took Buddhist wedding vows before not only Tai-san, but Yasutani Roshi, who happened to be visiting from Japan—an extremely fortuitous stroke of karmic coincidence, we were told.

We attended meetings at the Zen Studies Society for several months, listening to Yasutani Roshi's talks in translation, and then we moved to France. When we returned, the Zen Studies Society had moved into the beautiful, spacious East Side carriage house, and Soen Roshi had begun making periodic visits. The zendo became the cornerstone of our lives, and in 1974, Eido Roshi asked us to direct a summer residential program at Dai Bosatsu Zendo. At the end of that summer we stayed on. It was an exciting, pioneering time; we felt it a great privilege to take part in the shaping of American monastic Zen. We also worked with Eido Roshi on *Namu Dai Bosa: A Transmission of Zen Buddhism to America* (Theatre Arts Press), of which Lou was the editor; the book included teisho and poetry by Nyogen Senzaki and Soen Nakagawa, and an account by Eido Roshi of the events leading to the establishment of the New York Zendo and Dai Bosatsu Zendo.

In 1976, we moved to Syracuse, where Lou had been offered a position in the religion department at Syracuse University. The following year, we organized a national conference on Buddhism in America at the university; among the speakers we invited was Maurine. Her simple, straightforward presentation was memorable as a clear expression of Zen rather than a talk about it. At the end of that year, on the last day of Rohatsu sesshin, December 8, Maurine was ordained by Eido Roshi at Dai Bosatsu Zendo. He gave her the ordination name Chiko (Wisdom Light). With the encouragement not only of her teachers from the Zen Studies Society, but of her newfound friend and mentor, Elsie Mitchell, Maurine had been taking an increasingly important role in the development of Zen practice in New England. When she had first contemplated moving from New York to Boston with such unhappiness, Soen Roshi had assured her that if she made contact with Mrs. Mitchell, all would be well. The author of the 1973 book *Sun Buddhas Moon Buddhas,* Elsie Mitchell had visited Japan several times. The recordings of sutra chanting at Eihei-ji, the Soto temple founded by Dogen Zenji in 1244, that she and her husband, John Mitchell, had made on one of those trips were later released as the album *Zen Buddhist Ceremony* by Folkways Records. In 1957, the Mitchells helped establish the Cambridge Buddhist Association; that autumn, D. T. Suzuki and Shinichi Hisamatsu came to Cambridge. Dr. Hisamatsu taught at the Harvard Divinity School and conducted zazen at the CBA's library and zendo at 3 Craigie Street until his departure the following spring. Dr. Suzuki, who had been supported by the Zen Studies Society when he was teaching at Columbia University earlier that decade, remained for an extended visit, and was named president of the Cambridge Buddhist Association in 1959, a post he held (mostly in absentia) until his death in 1966. The association moved to 126 Brattle Street in 1971, the year Maurine and Elsie Mitchell met; in 1976, following the death of the Rev. Chimyo Horioka (who had succeeded Dr. Suzuki), Maurine was elected president and was also given complete charge of the Zen practice there.

Students had found Maurine even in her suburban home in Chestnut Hill, where a single cushion in a corner of her living room soon drew others; the group quickly outgrew that space, so Maurine set up a zendo in what had been a basement playroom. Once the two women met, it wasn't long before Mrs. Mitchell was relying on Maurine in many capacities, from leading zazen at the Cambridge Buddhist Association's library zendo to taking over the correspondence and the library responsibilities. All of this activity was a balm for Maurine's spirit; a warm rapport developed between the two, each of whom spoke of the other as her teacher. And Mrs. Mitchell was a most inconspicuous yet steadfast supporter: she made it clear that Maurine was not to worry about financial matters. If something was needed, it mysteriously appeared. Often, when I admired a dress Maurine wore on a trip to Syracuse, or the car she drove during my visits to Cambridge, she would smile, shake her head, and say, "That Elsie! She is so good to me."

In 1979, the CBA purchased a stately, three-storied, brown-shingled house surrounded by flower beds, pines, dogwoods, and birch trees at 75 Sparks Street in the beautiful Brattle Street area of Cambridge. Initially, there were problems with local residents, who seemed to fear that the Buddhist group was some kind of cult that would spirit away their children and cause their property values to plummet. A civil court ruled in favor of the CBA, and on June 12, 1980, a dedication ceremony was held. The schedule during that first year was arranged according to the needs of those who came to sit regularly. Soon a formal schedule of daily zazen and monthly sesshin was created, and people began coming to practice there from all over Massachusetts and from New Hampshire, Vermont, New York, and Canada. The number of students practicing with Maurine grew to more than four hundred during the ensuing years. She also was invited to California many times to conduct sesshin, several of which were for women only, women who felt wounded by intimate relationships with male teachers at various Buddhist centers.

Emphasizing that such a separatist approach could only be a temporary method of healing, Maurine steered clear of moralizing. Her own passionate response to life gave her reason to know that sexual energy could be a component in the complex dynamic between a teacher and a student, but she stressed that it was always the teacher's responsibility to act according to his or her compassionate understanding. For herself, she said, sex was not an appropriate teaching method. She also disagreed with those who insisted that truly enlightened teachers could not act in unenlightened ways; she pointed out that profound spiritual realization did not necessarily imply psychological clarity or the resolution of deep-seated emotional problems. For her, a teacher's failings were a reminder of what the Buddha had taught, Rinzai had taught, and Soen Roshi had taught: "Be a lamp unto yourself." "Don't put anyone else's head above your own." "Don't hang on me; I am just an ordinary person, an ordinary monk." Nevertheless, she spoke out against what she considered the principal failing: deception on the part of teachers unwilling to face the consequences of their actions.

After moving to Syracuse, I visited Maurine first in Chestnut Hill and later in Cambridge. Maurine and I would sit together, prepare meals, go to restaurants, visit museums, listen to music, and share books. All of this was wound through with seemingly free-flowing yet intently focused discussions. Although these were not Dharma dialogues in any obvious sense, I always knew she was seeing right into the depths of my being, and that it was fine. During the difficult period of my separation and divorce from Lou, her rock-solid presence wordlessly told me, "move on; move on." When I brought Andy Hassinger, my second husband, to meet her, she embraced him unquestioningly, open-heartedly.

Although she no longer practiced with Eido Roshi, in 1982 Maurine returned to Dai Bosatsu Zendo where, in a private encounter at the old lodge, Soen Nakagawa Roshi transmitted his Dharma to her. "Tell your students to call you Roshi," he said, and that was that: no ceremony, no authentication, no formal recognition, no lineage papers. He, in fact, said not a word about it to anyone else. It was perhaps his greatest koan for her: a transmission definitely "outside the scriptures," in keeping with his unconventional spirit.

How to communicate this formless transmission? What proof did she have? Immediately, rumors began flying, and there was no small degree of disgruntlement. Perhaps she had made the whole thing up, wanting some formal recognition? Perhaps this was simply another of Soen Roshi's eccentric acts, a mischievous test? No one knew quite how to receive this information, which quickly spread along the Dharma grapevine. As for Maurine herself, after dutifully communicating what Soen Roshi had asked her to, she told her students, "Please just call me Maurine." It was not in her nature to seek credentials or titles; she simply went on as she had before, wearing the same robes, keeping the same busy schedule of sesshin, daily zazen practice, piano recitals and lessons, spending time with her children, traveling. Yet increasingly one could sense a redoubtable power within this elegant lady with the leonine hair (now white) and strong, dark, arching eyebrows, who wore lipstick and foundation, who offered Bach instead of calligraphy.

On March 11, 1984, eight days before his seventy-seventh birthday, Soen Nakagawa Roshi died at Ryutaku-ji in Japan. As soon as I heard the news, I called Maurine; from our shared grief and our wish to do something in his honor came the arrangement that she would conduct a sesshin later that spring at the Zen Center of Syracuse. It was her first sesshin with us, and she left us glowing. During the ensuing years, my friendship with Maurine evolved into a student-teacher relationship. She made semiannual trips to Syracuse to lead sesshin, and I traveled to Cambridge as often as I could. My first sesshin at Sparks Street was in May 1985.

On December 8, 1985, on the last day of Rohatsu sesshin there, I was ordained by her, together with the senior student at the Cambridge Buddhist Association, Sheila LaFarge. The Dharma connection among the three of us was reinforced by the shared syllables of our Buddhist names. Maurine had received MyoOn (Subtle Sound) in 1968 from Soen Roshi, and Chiko (Wisdom Light) from Eido Roshi in 1977. She had given Sheila the Dharma name Myoko (Subtle Light), and Eido Roshi had given me the name Roko (Sparkling Dew). Now Sheila received the ordination name RoOn (Alert Hearing); I, Myochi (Subtle Wisdom).

In the wake of Soen Roshi's death, Maurine's Wisdom Light grew ever brighter. Turning her unflinching gaze on her personal life, she resolved to uproot all traces of self-deception. This included eliminating the glass or two of wine she had been relying on each evening to dull the painful recognition that her marriage was over. What resulted was a fierce clarity by which she was able to proceed with the very difficult yet necessary step of separation and eventual divorce from Ozzie.

When Maurine was diagnosed with cancer in 1987, she never exhibited a moment of self-pity or fear. If anything, the level of intensity at which she customarily lived was raised several notches. Plans had already been made to travel to India with a small group of students. She made the choice not to have the advised surgery and, despite the uncertainty about her condition, she went off and had a marvelous time conducting zazen under a descendant of the bodhi tree beneath which Shakyamuni Buddha had realized the fundamental birthlessness and deathlessness of it all.

She returned to months of medical tests, months of inconclusive evidence, and finally, months of growing weakness: still, sesshin after sesshin, Maurine gave of herself freely, wholeheartedly. She never seemed to pace herself, despite the fretful expressions of concern on the part of many of her students, her family, her friends. She brushed any attempts at commiseration aside; she refused to discuss her condition and she never complained, even toward the end, when she was hiding little notes to herself regarding the effectiveness and timing of various pain medications. Her demeanor was that of a fierce warrior-woman. Maurine sat through Rohatsu 1989 and the weekend sesshin of January 1990 with an all-but constant cough, with frequent nosebleeds, but she sat, nobly and fully present.

In my journal notes made during that Rohatsu, I wrote, "Maurine's talks seem to be preparing us for her death. During dokusan last night she told me, 'I have chosen a place under the birch trees in the back yard where I want my ashes spread.' This morning, she talked of Soen Roshi's pure, illuminating, radiant, childlike nature, and how it had evolved through great struggle; and said something I never knew before, that he had once contemplated suicide. She talked of his way of speaking of no-death, and that we take this form for a brief period, but that our energy continues as it had before our birth."

On the first day of sesshin, Maurine conducted a memorial service for a Vietnamese student's father. She said, "With this memorial service, we remember with tender reverence the members of our families who are no longer living. Let us realize that the ones whom we remember today existed before this birth. At that time they were without a body. Then substance was added to that spirit, and they were born. Let it be clear to us that the same process of change which brought them to birth eventually brought them to death, in a way as natural as the progression of the seasons. . . . May we remind ourselves that we are not to fall into a complacent state of mind where we are insensitive to suffering beings. Yes, we must cultivate a peaceful mind, firm and imperturbable. But we must keep the heart sensitive to the needs of others. The way is epitomized in the *Kannon Sutra.* Kannon grows arms without ceasing, to reach out to every cry for help. Let us try to extend this compassionate wisdom over the whole universe."

Living with cancer, Maurine was vibrantly, vigorously alive. When the time came to go, she opened her arms to death the way she had embraced every moment of her life. She entered the hospital in February 1990. The following weekend, twenty-five students, led by Billy Meegan, sat sesshin at Sparks Street. Dr. Masatoshi Nagatomi, then the vice president of the Cambridge Buddhist Association, came to visit Maurine that Saturday, February 24; that night, Billy and CBA resident Dennis Lennox stayed with Maurine in her hospital room. On the evening of February 25, Amie Diller, a West Coast student who had spent some time as a resident at Sparks Street the year before, flew in with her baby, Shauna Maurine Diller, Maurine's godchild. Maurine briefly drifted back to consciousness, saw them, and smiled. She passed away at 4 A.M. on February 26, surrounded by her children, Elaine, Barbara, and Marc. Her last words were, "Wonderful peace. Nobody there."

Maurine left no Dharma heir; her transmission was not by way of an established lineage, not to a select one or two. Her legacy was all-inclusive. Everyone who came into contact with her, whether as a Zen student or a piano student, a casual visitor or a family member, felt changed for having known her. Maurine was endlessly grateful to the many people in her life who had helped, encouraged, and supported her in her music and her Zen practice. To her Bodhisattva's vow was added the driving force of her sense of obligation. Teaching, imparting her own understanding to others, was her means of repaying those debts.

Health, Maurine taught us during those last months, is not the opposite of sickness. Although our habitual way of thinking is dualistic, in reality we are all living with good cells and bad cells simultaneously, in a condition of utter impermanence. She referred to the seventeenth-century Japanese monk Takuan Soho, who wrote one hundred poems he called "dream-poems." At the end of his life, he summoned his students and said, "After I've died, please bury my body in the mountain behind the temple; cover it with dirt; and go home. Read no sutras; hold no ceremony. Receive no gifts from either monks or laity. Let the monks wear their robes, eat their meals, and go on about their work as on normal days." Asked by his disciples for some last words, he said, "I have no last word." At his final moment, Takuan took up his brush, wrote the Chinese character for "dream," put down the brush, and died.

"This one character, dream," Maurine commented in one of her talks, "symbolized for Takuan the reality of the Dharma. It went beyond talking or not talking, is it or isn't it. Just a dream. When we realize that we and the universe are just a dream, when alive we are alive through and through, and everything around us is alive. Life is a dream, death is a dream, heaven and earth and all things under the sun, are just a dream."

In each aspect of her life, Maurine radiated her "dream": pure, clear, transparent. Her Zen was not reserved for the zendo, the lecture hall, or the conference room. It was expressed at the piano and at the stove, with her own children and with the children of her students, in restaurants and in concert halls. In every moment, in every place, she was always completely, vividly present.

She often spoke about her feelings of intimacy with Soen Roshi. After having "joined the majority" (his favorite expression for death), he was nonetheless right there for her. I now know what she felt. The form in which we knew her has disintegrated; the dream has dissolved; but MyoOn, Subtle Sound, reverberates on and on.

October 1995
Zen Center of Syracuse Hoen-ji
Syracuse, New York

NOTES

1. Ralph Waldo Emerson, in *Letters and Social Aims* (1875): "What you are stands over you the while, and thunders so that I cannot hear what you say to the contrary."
2. Helen Tworkov, *Zen in America* (San Francisco: North Point Press, 1989), p. 172.
3. The excerpt "My Childhood," from which this quotation was taken, was published in the Yasutani Memorial Issue of *ZCLA Journal,* vol. 3, nos. 3 and 4, Summer/Fall 1973, pp. 32–35.

Subtle Sound

1

The Illusion of "I"

SHAKYAMUNI BUDDHA taught many wonderful things, and he taught them according to the circumstances. He spoke according to the profession, the understanding, and the experiences of the person with whom he was speaking. When he talked to a poet, he spoke in and of poetry. When he talked to a mother, he talked about her children. Above all, he spoke of the unity of life everywhere, and of compassion for every living being. His teaching came from his own experience of the human condition, from his intuitive understanding of its essential character.

Buddhism embraces all religions, all traditions. We Buddhists have deep respect for every one of them, and realize that fundamentally, we are all one. We may use different phrases at different times, but we are all one.

This practice that we are engaged in is very down to earth and pragmatic. At the same time, it is preeminently of the spirit. It is a balanced and satisfying way of life, with feet firmly planted on the ground and heart open to the whole universe. This practice does not impose any creeds or dogmas upon us. It demands no blind faith, no submission to any separate deity or person or thing. This is an essential matter.

In Buddhism, all beings, without exception, are seen in the beauty and dignity of their original perfection, not their original sin. By our own efforts and intuitive insights we may uncover this perfection, which is our real and intrinsic Buddha-nature. This is enlightenment. Our Buddhist practice, deep and simple, is a way of life. It is a life-long study and practice—not only for this life, but for the next life, and the next, and so on. It can be a profound study, with inner meanings and depths endlessly expanding before us, and it can also be extremely simple, just teaching the basic ethical practices of daily living, practices of unselfishness, compassion, and good will toward every living being.

Buddhism emphasizes the transiency of all material things, and the illusory and impermanent nature of what we think of as our own personal ego. It also teaches the unity and kinship of all life. This practice involves mindfulness in every aspect of our lives. So it is, as Mumon says, like walking on the edge of a sword, over the ridge of an iceberg, with no steps, no ladders, climbing the cliffs without hands. There is no deviation from this path, this sword's edge, this ridge of the iceberg. We must be mindfully present with whatever difficult part of the path comes along.

Everything we do in the zendo—the arrangement of each object, the sitting in this wonderful posture, the walking with mindfulness—is exceedingly important. Not just in the zendo, but wherever we are, this mindfulness is important. Not to step on insects; to see if there is an impediment in the road and take care of it so somebody else doesn't fall; all of this is an extremely important part of our practice.

Then, of course, there is our meditation, our zazen. In awakening this intuitive mind, we awaken a deep compassion for all living creatures not as beings separate from ourselves, but as part of our own being, as we are of theirs. This, too, we feel in the zendo. We don't talk to one another, we don't gossip about things, we don't chat about the weather. We are sitting in deep silence, sensing what it is that belongs to every human being, animal, plant, tree, stone, the whole universe. And it makes us very compassionate and openhearted to one another, if we permit it. This is living practice.

Books are beautiful and inspiring. Lectures may help us. Scriptures are also important, but these are not enough. It's living practice that is most essential. Buddhism is not based on blind faith in anything that is written in any book, however holy. Even the preaching of Buddha himself is not to be treated in this way. The Buddha said, put no other head above your own. If it doesn't fit, don't do it.

What our practice is based on is right understanding. This is the first step on the Eightfold Path, obtained through reasoning, study, devotion, zazen, and the practice of selflessness and love. Some people think that Buddhism doesn't have much to do with love. It has everything to do with love. It just doesn't sentimentalize it. It doesn't get icky, or gushy, or oozy. It's very practical, this selflessness and love practice. Don't give me a long speech about love, but show me by your action what is in your heart. Don't weep sentimentally about something and the next minute crush an insect.

With deep practice, with more and more understanding, we come to realize that we are not punished for our sins. This is not part of our way of being. We are not punished for our sins, but by them. Whatever we do that is not loving, that is selfish, that is egocentric, that is grabby, comes home to roost. If we are in pain, if we suffer, we need to examine where it comes from. Probably it issues from some activity that is not unselfish, that is selfishly motivated. We suffer because we want so much, because we think that situations should be different from the way they are.

When we are chanting the Three Refuges—when we take refuge in the Buddha, in the Dharma, and in the Sangha—what are we doing? We take refuge in the Buddha: the Buddha was a great teacher. The historical Buddha may not ever have lived, but the presence that we think of as the Buddha, or Buddha, without the article, is a great teaching. We have not found somebody or something to make us feel secure. It's not a refuge in that sense. We are not hiding in the Buddha. Refuge is used as an example. The idea is that an ordinary human being came to an awakened state of mind by realigning himself to the situations around him. This is available to every single one of us. This human being disciplined himself by working on his own mind, which is the source of our chaos and confusion. We can't blame it on somebody else. We can't hide in something. We have to take full responsibility for this chaos and confusion, and if we really want to do something about it, we will.

When someone comes to me and says, "I don't really know how to integrate my practice into my work," I tell that person, "Don't try. Practice and work go together. If you feel that they are separate, you are bringing about a state of confusion. Whatever kind of practice you are able to engage in, however much or little, the quantity of it is not so essential. This extends itself into your work, and the quality of your work extends itself into your practice. There is no way to separate them. If you try to separate them, then you have chaos and confusion. Whatever you are doing, do it. Just do it."

Someone who practices archery told me, "I can stand up; I can do all the wonderful preparations; but when it comes to letting the arrow go, I can't do it." I said, "Stop the 'I' from doing it; just shoot." Thoughts of making a mistake, not hitting the target, being embarrassed in front of the teacher, these are what cause chaos and confusion. Let the 'I' go and just shoot. Let the 'I' go and just work. Let the 'I' go and just sit.

We take refuge in the Dharma. The Dharma is our path. Everything in our life is a constant process of learning and discovering. Everything in our life is to be related to fully. Everything is the path, constantly changing, constantly becoming something else. There is absolutely nothing that remains the same even for one minute. So we have many ups and downs, many waves in the ocean of our life. Taking refuge in the Dharma means that we relate fully to every single thing that happens.

We take refuge in the Sangha. We know how much it means to us to sit together. The atmosphere is created here by all of us. With our sincere attitude, we strengthen one another. We sit down here together and share a sense of trust. Somebody said, "But what if I cry in the zendo?" Then cry. You're in wonderful company. We all understand this feeling. "What if I laugh?" Laugh. You're in wonderful company. It may lighten all our hearts. We're not here to judge you, to say that's bad, you don't do that in the zendo. We trust one another, and we have a large-scale friendship. I may not see you for months at a time, but when I do see you, it's as if we just said hello five minutes ago, good-bye five minutes ago, and we're back again. We have this trust and this friendship, but at the same time we have to stand on our own two feet. We are working together, sitting together, helping each other, but not in a way that we become dependent on each other's help. That would be taking away something very important. We become independent, and then we can really depend on one another. We have a clean, clear friendship, without expectations and without demands.

Every day we chant the Four Great Vows. In chanting them, we are reminded again and again of what our work is. It is an impossible task. How can we sincerely vow to do what we cannot do? These vows are Buddhist vows, and in Buddhism there is the understanding that the "I" of "I vow," this intentional "I," is an illusion. So the first realization with these vows is that 'I' cannot undertake anything. And with this, the first step in our path is actualized. "I" is the obstacle; we get rid of it.

So now we put our palms together with a different attitude: not "I" vowing, but giving myself up to the carrying out of the vow. If this attitude of giving ourselves wholeheartedly and completely is truly practiced in whatever we are doing, the touchiness of "I," the stiffness of the ego, is softened. Just as we experience in sesshin, there is no thought of "I" doing anything. And in this softening, our suffering is decreased.

This softening is also the preparation for the working through of our passions, which we all have. Our emotional reactions, great or small, are aptly called in Buddhism "the fires"— the fire of sadness, the fire of loneliness, the fire of anger. With the attitude of giving ourselves, we can also give ourselves to the fires, rather than avoiding or refusing them or being carried away by them. Usually we refuse to come into contact with those fires, or we give in and are carried away by them, swept away. We are not willing to suffer their irrational force, and so it remains wild, and in need of humanizing. Neither refusing nor letting it rip: this is compassion for ourselves. Giving ourselves into the fires again, again, and again. They will consume "me," which is a real purification. They will consume the ego. With the absence of that ego, the fuel is gone, and the fires revert to what they have ever been: our own true Buddha-nature.

The central core of Buddhist practice is *anatta:* no "I." With this illusion of "I" gone, everything can be seen as it really is: different, but not separate. There is no clinging, no alienation; just a warm connection with what is. Buddha's teaching began with suffering and the way out of suffering. And he taught us through his own life, his birth, his awakening, and his death, the way out of loneliness, separation, and the fear of death. If there is no "I," if the shell of "I" is cracked, the liberation of the heart naturally shines forth, and acts in peace and joy for all beings.

This path, so clearly shown to us, is a way out of the illusion of "I," a way out of loneliness, separation, and fear of death. Only "I" can fear. Without "I," there is no fear. It says in the *Heart Sutra,* "No hindrance in the mind, therefore no fear." When that ego-shell is cracked, the wonderful warmth of the human heart is released. It is liberated; it shines, flows, acts. True Buddhist compassion warms and inspires us on the Way. True Buddhist wisdom lights our dark places and helps us out of our suffering; it helps us to feel peace and joy for all beings. At the end of the Bodhisattva's Vow, we chant, "May we extend this mind over the whole universe, so that we and all beings together may attain maturity in Buddha's wisdom." What is our Zen practice, if not this?

2

Ordinary Mind

S OMEBODY SAID TO ME, "It says in the precepts that I should not become intoxicated. I am intoxicated by zazen!" Indeed. This is a wonderful addiction. Drench yourself in it. Drink as much as you like. More, more, more! With this kind of intoxication, we become more in touch with everything. Literally and figuratively, our senses become very keen: we smell, taste, and touch with a new kind of awareness, and the intuitive mind becomes more sensitive as well. We find that there is less confusion in our lives; that we are more wide awake. By committing ourselves completely to our zazen, by accepting everything just as it comes, we become freer, more open, more alert, more vividly alive. Sparkling.

Each of us contributes in our own way. Working at whatever is given us to do with mindfulness and gratitude to this practice, we just do it, with our whole being. This place is glitteringly clean as a result. And this makes our practice go more clearly, sesshin go more smoothly. This is our zazen really going into daily life: clearly offering ourselves for the sake of all sentient beings, and grateful to all sentient beings for what they are doing. "Let us pray that all beings may accomplish whatever

tasks they are engaged in," we say every morning after break-
fast, "and be fulfilled with all the Buddha-dharmas."

In drenching ourselves in this zazen bath, we are giving up
our fixed positions, giving up our past, our thoughts of the future. We are just here, eating the food of the moment, bite after
bite. We know there are no quick solutions to our personal
koans; no sidetracks; no quick exits. We cannot blame our problems or our relationships on somebody else. We have to take full
responsibility, sitting here with ourselves. Nobody can do this
for us.

We seek security, we seek peace of mind, but we cannot grasp
anything; everything is continually changing. When we see this,
we are no longer bound by the need for security. We are suspended here in a place in which the only thing to do is to get in
touch with the teachings and ourselves. The only place in which
to begin is within ourselves. Nobody can do this for us. Nobody
can carry our packages. Nobody can carry our burdens. We have
to work with the richness of our own experience in everyday life.

We only know whether things are cool or warm when we
experience them ourselves. Somebody else can't say to us,
"That's cold." We must taste it, feel it. We cannot take the re-
ports of other people's experience as our own. If you put your
hand on your heart, it does not beat because you think about
making it beat. Nor do you need a medical definition of what a
heart is. A power beyond definition is making it beat. The basis
of our Zen practice is the reality of our life, which goes beyond
all definitions, beyond any words. That reality cannot be buck-
led up in a definition. We can't put it in a little pigeonhole and
say, "There, I have it neatly tucked away."

We are responsible for ourselves, as followers of the Dharma.
The path and the inspiration are up to each one of us. As far as
our way is concerned, human beings are extremely important.
But we must not interfere with one another. We must have wisdom as well as compassion in our actions. What is this compas-

sion? Somebody told me he had heard stories about how lacking in compassion Zen practice in Japan was; that it was so cold and austere. This does not seem to me to be what Zen is about. Compassion and wisdom, *karuna* and *prajna,* are our practice. One without the other is no good. Compassion without wisdom is mushy. Wisdom without compassion is cold.

How do we show compassion? Com-passion: with passion, with fire, with energy, with life. A very simple way to show our compassion is to leave the bathroom clean, so that the next person who comes finds a wonderful place. We don't leave a little sign there saying, "I did this for you"; it's just done, and there is that clean place. Another way to show compassion is to do our work completely, on our own, for the sake of the persons who come after us. We are independent and dependent on one another, and each one of us must be as clear as possible about our condition; then we may be depended upon.

I read a story about a monk who applied for acceptance to a monastery. While sitting in front of the monastery gate, he saw somebody coming up the road with a big package. He jumped up from his place by the gate and rushed down to take the package from that person, and the abbot of the monastery expelled him on the spot. Does that seem uncompassionate? This is a story to tell us that we must each carry our own stuff, and grow and learn from it, and ripen. When we are sitting at the gate, if we are ripe, we will know when to offer help and when to allow the person to carry his or her own burden, do his or her own work. We are here to help one another, to support one another, but not to interfere, and not to take on someone else's pain or burden. We feel one another's pain, since we are of one body, one mind, but we must allow each other our own experience, and contribute in our own way.

We are here to get rid of confusion about such matters. And it is entirely up to each one of us to dispel that confusion. What does it mean to have compassion? What does it mean to have wisdom? Our practice is one of intuitive awareness. It's not a matter of calling some rule up, saying, "It is the fifth precept I must follow here." What does the occasion ask from us? In the spontaneity and creativity of Zen, we see what really exists. Opinions merely clog things up; we lose the essence when we judge. When we see what is in front of us, we experience this ordinary mind, this radiant, spontaneous, ordinary mind on the Way.

While sitting in zazen, if we let go of our bodies, remove our minds, what do we have? A clear, pure condition free from delusions. In this condition, we are like a flash of lightning: free to come, free to go, free to feel pain, free to grow old, free to die, free to express our Zen in our own way, to express our Buddha-nature in everything we do, think, speak, and act. It sounds idyllic, doesn't it?

Our zazen practice requires intense *nen,* or present-mind. But to this nen we add the Bodhisattva's Vow, that we and all beings *together* may attain true wisdom. With this vow, our dualistic, discriminating mind disappears. We no longer think, "*I* am doing this work. *I* am doing this practice. This is *my* practice." All of this melts, and we come to feel that subject and object, in-breath and out-breath are one. We inhale the whole universe, exhale to the whole universe; there is no gate between us and it.

All Zen stories are about the same thing. There are different scenes, different characters, but they all help us see more clearly into our true nature, our Buddha-nature, the ground of our being—whatever we want to call it. Koans and rituals do not just pertain to ancient times; we must not let them become mere forms. We must be careful not to treat the old like dregs from the past, and not to see the new as imitations. When truly alive people make use of these koans, they become vividly present; distinctions between old and new are gone. Each koan is *our* koan. We must come forth in solitary freedom, independently. The clarification of the true self is none other than this practice we are engaged in. No one can teach us about it, no one can give it to us. We must find out for ourselves, clearly and inde-pendently.

3

Nothing Extraneous

I<small>N ANCIENT TIMES</small>, one of the most important pieces of equipment for a monk was the long staff. It was used when going on a pilgrimage; it was used when crossing a river to test the depth of the water, or to scatter insects that otherwise might be trodden upon and killed. But this staff, when it is referred to in Zen stories, is not just a piece of wood. This staff is our essential nature. It expresses the essential world.

Now, if you think you have something called essential nature, you are wrong. Such a concept is not true realization. If you think you have no essential nature, that it is completely empty, you must have that concept taken away, too.

We must go beyond these concepts of right and wrong, being and not-being, having and not-having. In the essential world, the world of *Mu,* there is no such thing as this opposed to that. In the New Testament, it says, "Unto him who hath, more shall be given to him. Unto him who hath not, even that which he hath shall be taken away." I used to have some thought about this: that it meant unto him who hath, if we truly understood this matter deeply, more will be given, and unto him who hath not, who does not understand, even that which he hath becomes tasteless. But I now think there's something else in the phrase "unto him who hath not": when we have given up everything, when everything has dropped away, then what?

How does this staff help us test the water of life? How deep is it? How do we get across it? This staff may become a dragon and swallow up the whole universe, as Ummon says. But if you hold on to even one little tiny thought about this staff, you will fall. There can be no separation between you and it. This staff is nothing other than ourselves. It is nothing other than the whole universe: *One*derful.

How are we practicing zazen? Even when we have been sitting for a long time, going to a beginners' instruction class is very helpful. Let's start again at the very beginning. We are always beginning. The rules for zazen have been handed down for generations from our Zen ancestors, who found the best way through their experience, but it's a good idea to review these rules every so often. Here is rule number one: we who are sitting here, we Zen students, must have compassion for all beings, and a deep longing to save all of them. We are not practicing zazen only for our own emancipation. Mahayana Buddhism, which is the way of the bodhisattva, is a layperson's Buddhism. We are practicing in the midst of daily life, in society, our businesses, our homes. When you look at pictures of bodhisattvas, they usually have long hair, and they're wearing ornaments such as necklaces, earrings, bracelets; these are the symbols of bodhisattvas who are laypeople.

Rule number two tells us that to achieve emancipation, we need to be free from distractions and disturbances, so that body and mind are one, movement and stillness are not separated. We don't eat too much or too little. We use a cushion of just the right height for our own posture, and we sit in an orderly atmosphere. Crossing our legs in the lotus or half-lotus posture, we then place the right hand on the left foot, palm up, and the left hand, palm up, on the right palm, and lightly touch our thumbs together. We begin by gently swaying from left to right to find our own balance, and then sitting straight, not leaning forward or backward. The bones of the hips are back, the vertebrae stacked one upon another like a stupa.

When we practice zazen we give up everything. We give up thoughts. Of course they come, but when they do, we give them up. We give up wanting something from our zazen. We give up any idea of becoming enlightened. To become enlightened is the most important thing in our lives, but to have thoughts about it is no good. We give up all extraneous thoughts about our sitting. We forget all matters that are extraneous to just sitting. When they come, we give them up. And we don't move! When the body moves, the mind follows; when the mind moves, the body follows. We harm our practice when we move. We have to start all over again. So we take the time to set up our posture, and then we sit absolutely still.

Our sleep must be regulated as part of our practice. Neither too little nor too much—the middle way, in every case, should be followed. Not getting enough sleep can make us crazy. Sitting with intensive nen is wonderfully productive. So sleep deeply when you sleep, not too much and not too little.

And we need to read. There are many wonderful books that can inspire us. People don't read enough. They think there's something wrong with reading, that it's not good for their practice. That's ridiculous. Reading is very helpful, very inspiring.

In the *Blue Cliff Record,* we read about the stone bridge of Joshu. A monk comes to Joshu and says all he sees is a simple log bridge, not the renowned stone bridge. Why can't the monk see it? The stone bridge is the ever-functioning, dynamic spirit of Zen in action, which has been transmitted from heart to heart, mind to mind, from generation to generation. This is what we are here to see: this stone bridge. Do we just see an old plank? What is our Zen understanding? What is our deep experience of this? Each of us has within ourselves this true Buddha-nature. We are here to experience it. Without the enlightened mind, there is no Zen. So we have a deep responsibility to wake up, not with anxiety that there must be something wrong with us because we haven't gotten it, but with an open-hearted attitude—with open *haras*. We drop off all extraneous matters and just do zazen; just let zazen do us, with absolutely meticulous attention. Attention! Attention! Attention! Nothing more, nothing less.

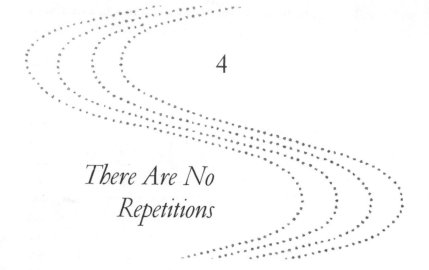

4

There Are No Repetitions

W HAT IS the condition of our minds right now? How are our hearts? This moment is all we have—so at this moment, how creative are we, how in touch with the source are we?

We need courage to be creative. To be sensitive and aware requires great courage. This word "courage" comes from the same root as the French word "coeur," which means heart. So please have the courage to listen to your heart, to your body, your hara, not just to your head. You will discover new ways to experience your life.

We are always at the beginning. It is always the very first time. Truly, there are no repetitions. When I play the piano, I often come to a repeat sign. Can that passage be repeated? If I am teaching a piano student and we see a repeat sign, I tell the student that there are no repeats. We return to the beginning of a certain passage, but it's never the same. It's always fresh. Someone asked me, "Don't you get tired of answering the same questions day after day—what is Zen, how do we practice?" Never! It's never the same question, because it's always coming from a different person, in a different moment; and each person asks the question from his or her own state of mind. The words may sound alike, but each time they are coming from somewhere unique.

What is zazen? Hui-neng defined zazen this way: "In the midst of all good and evil, not a thought is aroused in the mind. This is called 'za.' Seeing into one's self-nature and not being moved at all, this is called 'zen.' " We sometimes say "za" is just to sit cross-legged, but it means more than this; it means to sit with no discriminating consciousness, no dualistic activity. And "zen" is to wake up to our fundamental self, not to be disturbed by anything—just letting it come, letting it go; in-breath, out-breath; just here. Allowing the calm, deep breath to penetrate every part of the body, allowing the hara to fill up, we let go of all fixed notions. We let go of "I." We let it all fall off. We are here to discover a way of relating to one another, rather than to expound a set of doctrines. With this attitude, our sitting is receptive, alert, awake, open, so that we can hear what the silence has to say. We are letting ourselves be the vehicle for whatever teaching may come our way, not forcing or grabbing at anything.

Because I consider myself an artist, I tend to think in terms of poetry and music, but above all, it is the art of our own life that we are engaged in. The greatness of a poem or a painting is not that it portrays a certain scene or experience, but that it shows the artist's vision of his or her own meeting with reality. Hence each thing, each time, is fresh and new. It is never the same place. There are no repetitions. It is not the head or the hand that paints the picture or performs the sonata. One of my teachers gave me a wonderful koan: "Play the piano without using your hands." When we are empty and free, then the brush or the notes move by themselves. This is the source, whether or not we call it Zen, that we are in touch with. Is it done by heaven, or is it our doing? Our doing is heaven's. Our movements are heaven's. If the artist interferes, or if we as artists of our lives interfere with this source through some self-conscious preoccupation, what happens? What is to be expressed gets lost, becomes hard, constrained; there is no true expression. When mind and heart are open, empty; when there is no selfish motivation; then all one's actions are one with heaven. The spirit flows freely, and we have a heavenly dance.

On loan to us at the Cambridge Buddhist Association for awhile was a most extraordinary calligraphy, by Soen Nakagawa Roshi. The top character, "human," was very still. The bottom character was a wonderful swirling energetic character: "Heaven-dance." This heaven-dance comes through all of us when we let go of all our ego-stuff, when we melt down the ego and let this source move freely through us.

In Japanese culture, the creative process is described by words like *ki,*—vital energy; *kan,*—transcendent intuition; and *myo,*—wondrous action. When energy strikes intuition, a wondrous sound emerges. Myo also refers to a certain artistic quality not only in works of art, but in anything in our lives, in nature. This myo is something original, creative, growing out of one's own consciousness, one's own experience: spontaneous and personal creativity.

We speak of the wonders of nature. Nature is full of myo. Nature is always showing this unfathomable, absolutely inexhaustible myo, and there are many wonderful poets who express this to us. Basho, who was the role model for Soen Nakagawa, who in turn was the great inspiration for my life, wrote wonderful poems of nature, but they are not just nature poems; they richly convey this myo. Here are two examples:

> Stillness
> penetrates the rocks
> cicadas chirp

> The temple bell dies away
> but the fragrance of flowers resounds—
> evening

Such elegance! By the way, this word, elegance, is also used by physicists to describe their discoveries. Basho has given us a glimpse of the source. To come to such elegance, to come to such feeling, doesn't happen by taking some pill, or some magic potion, but through strong discipline. This is not only true of Zen practitioners, but of all great artists. How many times did Beethoven write, rewrite, tear up, sort out all the things that came to his mind, day by day, week by week, month by month, until he finally distilled everything down to the wonderful sound we hear at this point! How many times do artists draw, draw again, over and over again, perfecting their technique so that they may work freely and directly from this source. We can speak very easily about how we should be free, how we should empty our minds, how we should open our hearts, but to do this, we need strong practice. As musicians we practice hour after hour perfecting a phrase so that we may have some freedom of expression when it comes time to give it to someone else. As Zen practitioners we sit in zazen, hour after hour, day after day, year after year, refining our minds and spirits, to come to this elegance, to come to this place where we can be what Rinzai called the true person of no rank, or what Dogen called the primordial person: one who has freely dropped off the ego-self. Basho described this condition in another haiku:

> Along this road
> goes no one
> this autumn evening

We are the no-person person, and at the same time, we are doing what needs to be done, completely, fully, absolutely, concentratedly.

We must be completely present with whatever we are doing—so completely present that there is no separation between it and us. Sitting on the cushion is relatively easy. To take it into everyday life, to be completely mindful of what we are doing, this is more difficult—and essential. We must make our base very strong, like the Daruma doll—no matter how many times he's knocked down, he pops right up again. We are doing mindfulness practice to nourish this fundamental source of our being.

We have this source within us, but we must do our practice over, and over, and over; sit over and over, do whatever tasks we are engaged in over and over. Yet nothing is repeated. It's hard to keep wide awake, to keep vividly present in the midst of endless repetition. But look at this! Taste this! We may have drunk a million cups of tea, but we have never tasted this one before.

5

Giving It Away

I T'S EASY TO SAY, "Just become simple, plain, ordinary. Don't think about the past or the future, just live in the present moment." How difficult! Practicing together, we learn more and more, moment to moment, that we cannot apply what worked in the past to this time. This is completely different. Everything must be done in a fresh, present-tensed way. The old rules don't apply. We must pay attention to what the present moment asks of us. When the future that we expected is here, it may be entirely different from what we envisioned. So what is the use of all that worrying about how to deal with it?

Hui-neng tells us we will never grasp anything by thinking about it after it has happened. If our minds are clear, we will see our original nature at this moment. If our minds are not fuzzy, not painted over by some fixed ideas, not held in thrall by old ways, old traditions, our original nature can be seen immediately. Hui-neng also says that if we hold onto an evil thought we will destroy the cause of a million years' virtue. What does he mean by an evil thought? One such thought that causes us all a lot of pain is resentment. It may make us feel quite superior to say to someone, "I forgive you." Things quiet down, perhaps, but the pain and resentment may be pushed down into our unconscious minds, and a rigidity comes to the surface. We may say, "I'll never do that again." But how do we know what we will or will not do again?

True forgiveness brings a great change in our hearts. We are always talking about openheartedness. Again, it is easy to talk about, but difficult to do. What is it to truly open our hearts in forgiveness? It is to see all the blows of fate we have experienced, all the rejections of the past, present, and future, all our weaknesses, as part of a darkness that has helped to bring us more light.

We are engaged in a practice of looking in the mirror, seeing ourselves clearly, seeing what is real and what is an illusion. "How can I extend my Zen practice to all my friends?" someone asked me. We cannot do anything but allow the fruits of the practice to come through us, in our spontaneous response to whatever is asked of us, wherever we go. Just unself-consciously and spontaneously responding to circumstances with an open heart and mind: this is our practice. It is the only thing that we can do. We cannot plan to extend our Zen practice to this person, to that country. Who knows what will be asked of us, here, there, or anywhere? We don't just decide that we're going to bring our Zen practice into our lives. Our practice *is* the foundation of our lives. We cannot unearth the root and say, "This is what I'm going to live by." Zazen is the root. It is what we are experiencing day by day, through our bodies as much as through our minds. We can memorize all the sutras and shastras, we can read innumerable books, we can search for some key phrase we think will enlighten us because we have read that Hui-neng was enlightened when he heard the *Diamond Sutra*. We may try to grasp all these words, but eventually we will forget them. What we never forget is what our bodies have learned. Our bodies remember what they experience. They hurt in certain places to teach us something. If we allow the breath to go through the entire body, it naturally sits up straight. We don't have to fix it;

we just have to pay attention. Our bodies teach us through pain, through weariness, about what we are resisting. Why are we so rebellious that we get this little knot here or there? Why do we fall asleep? Why do we become bored during zazen? It's usually because we are really afraid to find out who we are.

To sit together in the zendo is paradise. During sesshin, when your knees are hurting, you may not think so, but what a wonderful opportunity it is to be here together in this clean, clear stillness, with everyone completely participating, with delicious food offered to us three times a day. All you need to do is to let everything drop off, to deeply experience what we have here together, and then to take it home with you. All I can do is to encourage you, sit with you, hit you when you ask for the keisaku, insist that everything is meticulously taken care of in the house, maintain a strong atmosphere. The rest is up to you. So please, let go of all those contradictory concepts; wash them all away. And remember that this zazen mind is not some trance-like state in which you zoom off into the stratosphere. You don't lose consciousness, you remain absolutely present. You just give up your discriminating mind and become absolutely clear, wide awake. That is what *bodhi* means: enlightened, awakened, wide awake.

When Rinzai received a very distinguished visitor who asked him if his monks read the sutras, he replied, "They do not." Then the visitor asked if they practiced Zen. Rinzai said, "No, they do not practice Zen." The visitor did not understand, and asked, "Well then, what in the world are they doing here?" Rinzai answered, "All I have them do is become Buddhas and patriarchs." Zen is not something that is to be practiced, in the sense of practicing for what is coming up, what lies ahead. Zen is now. It lives; it's here. The sutras aren't read; Zen isn't learned. The sutras and Zen are directly penetrated with every pore of our being. Rinzai tells us not to get stuck in names and phrases; that even if we master a hundred sutras and shastras, we are not as good as one "who has nothing to do." This does not mean that we should not read, study, and absorb the sutras, but that in reading them, we should become them. We shouldn't seek some secret word or passage that we think will emancipate us, but instead just become one with what we read.

After his great enlightenment, Rinzai returned to his teacher, Obaku, to pay his respects. Obaku felt something was lacking; he needed to deepen Rinzai's understanding. So he hit him, hard. This was more than just striking him with his stick or with his hand; this was going deep, going beneath the skin. With one direct, intimate blow, he chased him out of the room. Rinzai could not understand why he was struck. He thought, "Here I have had such a wonderful experience and have come back to pay my respects to my teacher; why does he hit me?" But something deep within him responded, and he stayed on to finish out the training period. After it was over, he went to take his leave, and Obaku asked him, "Where are you going?" Rinzai's answer, "If I don't go to Ho-nan, then I'll return to Ho-pei," had nothing to do with north, south, east, or west. He meant that he was free to go anywhere: free to go, free to sit. Obaku understood this, and hit him again. This was a different kind of blow.

There are all kinds of hits; there are all kinds of intimate contacts in our lives. Sometimes a terrible blow wakes us up. Sometimes a blow is an expression of endearment. This time, Obaku struck him a parting hit, expressing his acknowledgment that Rinzai should go forth in order to awaken others. He was happily letting him set out on this journey of compassion, in which he would freely encounter everyone.

Obaku called his attendant and asked for his backrest and armrest. These things were symbolic of the transmission of the Dharma. Obaku had received them from Hyakujo Ekai as his Dharma heir. But what did Rinzai do? He asked the attendant to bring some fire, so he could burn them up. Who needed them? What a wonderful Zen spirit. Burn them up! This living

Dharma is sparkling everywhere. No need for some sign that I have it or you have it.

It is said that Shakyamuni's bowl and robe were transmitted down through the ages to Hui-neng, the Sixth Patriarch, at which point they were lost, thank goodness. Their loss is significant. Much harm has come from being overly concerned with transmission. These symbols and certifications have become hindrances. What sort of proof are they, anyway? We don't need a paper certifying our awakened state. True awakening fills the whole universe. Acknowledgment in Zen is different from receiving a diploma from a university. People often ask me, "What koans have you passed? Did you do all 1,700 koans?" This matter of acknowledgment in Zen is very precious, very intimate, and is not something to discuss.

To take this transmission from mind to mind, heart to heart and to transmit it is to give it away. It is to radiate it to the whole universe, without saying one word about having or not having. There is a saying, "Do not walk in the shadow of your teacher." This means that we must have our own insight. And in the *Rinzai Roku* it tells us that one's own insight must surpass that of one's teacher in order to be worthy. This doesn't mean in any competitive sense; it simply means that in addition to all the wonderful insights we have received from our teachers, we must have our own deep understanding.

Every day is a fresh day. In our strong, grounded zazen posture, we are dynamically composed. We are going directly to what has to be done. We are cutting off all extraneous matters with no blinking, no hesitation. We are just inquiring of ourselves, as Rinzai did, "Who is this noble person, this true person without rank? What is our original face before our parents were born?" Such words are not necessary, of course. "Who am I?" Even that is unnecessary.

Everyday life is our religion. The trees, the flowers, the stones are our Sangha. It is difficult to treat everyday life with the same respect that we accord each other during sesshin, but this mind accompanies us wherever we are, whatever we are doing. In the midst of the most confusing turmoil, in the midst of heartache, in the midst of sickness, whatever it is *is* our true practice.

6

Our One and Only Commandment

BEFORE THE TIME of Hui-neng, who lived in China during the T'ang dynasty, it had been thought that the experience of enlightenment could only be attained after one had practiced and attained some depth in *dhyana,* meditation. Perhaps some of us still think that. Hui-neng, however, maintained that prajna, transcendental wisdom, is inseparable from dhyana. Neither can be understood without the other.

There are three forms of discipline in our practice. The first is *sila,* moral precepts against stealing, gossiping, coveting, etc. The second is dhyana, or Zen, and the third is prajna. Hui-neng said that for true understanding, we must know that dhyana is not different from prajna, and that prajna is not something attained after practicing Zen. When we are practicing, in this very moment of practicing, prajna is unfolding itself in every single aspect of our lives: sweeping the floor, washing the dishes, cooking the food, everything we do.

This was the very original teaching of Hui-neng, and it marked the beginning of true Zen Buddhism. Everything is teaching us, everything is showing us this wonderful Dharma light. All we have to do is open our eyes; open our hearts. While we are doing, thinking, and feeling, Zen is there, prajna is there. This intuitive mind infuses everything we do. But this is not something about which we can have discursive knowledge. We cannot attain realization of this in that way. This intuitive knowledge comes from our body and our mind. We don't sit here and think about what enlightenment is. To think "I must get enlightened" is the greatest impediment. To have some degree of enlightenment is wonderful; to think about it is terrible. "No knowing" is what we do, as in the famous phrase of Bodhidharma. When the emperor of China asked, "Who is this who stands before me?" Bodhidharma replied, "No knowing." No knowing. There is no way that we can take this intuitive mind and quantify it. We can't say, "Here it is, I'm going to give you one month's worth, or two months' worth; now we've progressed to six months' worth, and now your course is finished." That's not it. We may see it in an instant, or it may take several lifetimes. This is a practice of endurance and patience. Forgetting all about gaining anything, we are simply trying to see clearly.

What does this seeing clearly mean? It doesn't mean that you look at something and analyze it, noting all its composite parts; no. When you see clearly, when you look at a flower and really see it, the flower sees you. It's not that the flower has eyes, of course. It's that the flower is no longer just a flower, and you are no longer just you. Flower and you have dissolved into something way beyond what we can even say, but we can experience this. This kind of seeing, this kind of understanding is "as-it-is-ness." This wonderful intuitive wisdom infuses everything we do, if we just open ourselves up to it, and forget about all our selfish petty concerns, forget about what we want, what we must get, whether this is doing something for us. Forget it. We are here for the sake of all sentient beings, and we are one with all sentient beings when we come to see this as-it-is-ness. Meister Eckhart, a thirteenth-century Christian mystic who really understood this, said, "The eye with which I see God is the same eye with which God sees me."

We see all things through the conceptualizing of color and form, and yet we do not see them in their true essence, because we separate ourselves from what we see. When we think of something as good or bad, it is our own habit of thought. It is because we have so much attachment to this discriminating mind that we do not experience Mu. It even shows in our bodies. We have something blocked somewhere, something that refuses to let go. We're so attached, even to pain. "That is *my* pain!" Whose pain? When you hear the *han* struck, do you feel the pain of the wood? Can you let go of your own pain, give up this imagined individual self, and just dissolve into *Muuuuu?*

Each of us is sometimes laughing, sometimes crying, and we are endlessly thinking of things. What about paying attention to what it is that makes us feel and think this way? We train our minds by looking into them. We just look in, not allowing ourselves to be carried away by our perceptions; we just look into what is going on, and ask, "Where does this come from?" We are training ourselves in the practice and study of Buddhism so that our thoughts and emotions do not disturb our true-nature mind, so that we can sit imperturbably no matter what.

Those of us who traveled to India together had the wonderful experience of sitting every day under the Bodhi tree with Tibetan monks chanting beside us, with people doing prostrations beside us, with children playing around us, with the whole world humming around us. We sat imperturbably, and some of us learned for the first time what it means to sit.

Hui-neng had an awakening when he heard the words from the *Diamond Sutra,* "Depending on nothing, realize your own mind." We are so often depending on this religion or that, this "ism" or that. Don't even think about Buddhism. The true Buddhist never says, "I am a Zen Buddhist." We are people who are practicing this universal principle with everybody in the whole cosmos. There is no label, no separation, no statement like "I am Buddhist, he is Christian. "True Buddhism embraces the whole universe, without a single label. You must have your own experience of the study and practice of Buddhism, not think thoughts that have been given to you by anybody else, including myself. Forget everything I have said. Depend on yourself. Your own experience of your inner self is what this is about.

Through clarifying our minds we can abandon our delusions and enlighten ourselves. Realizing we are a part of the whole universe, not separate, our minds become as clear as crystal, and all the Dharma is revealed. So let us see clearly; let us put all the past aside and go deeply into this, moment after moment. How do we do it? Just by our own natural breathing. If we try to slow the breath down, it becomes awkward and uncomfortable. Instead, we can narrow the breath. When we exhale, we narrow the exhalation, in what is called "bamboo breath." When we inhale, we don't take in a great gulp of air, but just a little, just enough. By breathing like this, more air is retained in the lungs, and quite naturally the breathing slows down. The transition from inhalation to exhalation becomes smoother; sitting becomes joyful. It is an immeasurable pleasure just to breathe in zazen.

Just to breathe, just to see clearly: this is the real meaning of the precepts. To keep the precepts does not mean following a set of rules. It is giving ourselves to a way of life, a path of compassionate action that expresses itself in everything we do. Our practice of zazen purifies and warms the mind so that the precepts are not really necessary. We have certain rules of behavior, of course. We get up in the morning; we wash, we dress mindfully; we straighten our cushions, we pay attention to our posture and our breath. Zazen practice itself is a precept—one of them, and at the same time, all of them. Dhyana is prajna. Everything is contained in what we are doing. This is our zazen, and this is our everyday life, every minute. So the power of this practice we are engaged in helps us keep the precepts without self-consciously trying to follow a set of rules. If we try to do it, if we think about it, if we read the list of precepts every morning and say, "Now, I mustn't do this, and I mustn't do that," it doesn't work. If it comes from the hara, from the intuitive wisdom mind, then it can be done. We can control ourselves very well when we are without any idea of controlling at all. There is nothing to do; there is nothing to control, nothing to follow. Without trying to do something, we simply practice, in the same way as when we are hungry, we eat; when we are tired, we rest. The precepts are not some rigid formulation outside ourselves.

There are a few Buddhist sects in which very strict precepts are observed. Some Buddhist monks could not come here because I am a woman. They could not come near a woman, let alone shake hands with her. I respect them, and they should not violate their commandments; if they find some deep meaning in them, that's fine. But in our practice, our one and only commandment is the intuitive response to our lives, and if we pay absolute attention to this, it is really difficult to violate.

7

Breathing In,
Breathing Out

WHEN WE ARE praised, we are happy. When we are blamed, we are unhappy. Even an old person such as myself loves to hear kind words, and is unhappy when somebody says something unpleasant to me. Supposedly wise, supposedly enlightened, I still have a need to be liked. We are all the same.

Koans, stories that originated in China, are transmitted from one to another of us to keep alive the spirit of Zen. But there are wonderful twentieth-century koans, and, in fact, the koans of our own lives are the best koans. What are we doing with the infinite resources that have been given to us? How are our lives taking shape?

How do we react to praise or criticism? Do we take criticism, or do we shrink from it when it is hard? Do we want more and more if we are praised? Are we greedy? We are constantly examining one another. When we know we are being observed, we often worry about being judged. This can be an impediment; it can make us feel very self-conscious, and become tight and constricted. But sometimes we are very aware of one another, aware of being observed, and we learn a great deal. To really be with a friend, to really be present to all the various shades and meanings of our lives together—how are we sharing this? How are we accepting this together?

Sometimes a teacher sees that praise can give a student confidence, and that he or she needs to be helped along. But sometimes it is necessary to criticize: "Not yet, go on, move on, don't get stuck here." As parents, we know how necessary this has been in bringing up our children. Sometimes it's important to be encouraging; sometimes we need to say, "That's no good, let's get on with this."

Nansen said, "If you are fooled by others, you will never get This Matter." Who are the others? Not other people, but all the other delusions that come up in our minds—those others that are not our true self. This Matter has nothing to do with whether it is fine or terrible, good or bad, black or white. It is beyond all that.

We are here to let go. We are not here to get something, but to let go of everything. We sit together to deeply understand This Matter, the ground of our being. Some people may say, "I'm sitting because I want to get some kind of peace of mind." Yet this is what gives us peace of mind: to experience the depths of ourselves and to understand that it belongs to all of us. So we walk together, harmoniously in step with each other. We work together as one body. We sit together and we feel this peaceful condition, this room that is filled with silence.

But when we get up from zazen, what happens? There is still fear, doubt, anxiety; there are innumerable thoughts that assault us. So year after year we sit, and we become more stable, so that the inevitable difficulties that come up in our lives do not shake us, do not knock us off our rockers. To enter into this unshakable state of being is to see things just as they are: rain as rain, wind as wind, anger as anger, joy as joy—everything, just as it is. If this is our condition, then we are not being fooled by others, we are not being fooled by all the junk that clutters up our minds; we are not regretting, not daydreaming, not wishing things were otherwise.

Our practice never comes to an end. There are endless steps along the way. Even the most outstanding Zen masters are taking endless steps. And with each step, the circumstances of our lives are asking, "Are you here? Are you present?" What is it that impedes us? How seriously are we taking our own individual and separate selves? Too seriously, most of the time. To live with our consciousness rooted in this present-minded condition is to lose our self-important seriousness and to live more playfully. Buddha-nature, the essence of it all, we take supremely seriously, but not this passing form.

How do we live this way? How do we begin? When sitting, just sit. When walking, just walk. To think over what has just gone on or to wonder what is to come or to think about how it will affect us is to lose the moment. We can get so caught up in such concerns that we live our lives secondhand. If we are so much *with* what we are doing that there is no room for anything else, then we are in direct contact with the flow of our lives, with the flow of Buddha-nature in us, working through us.

If you are a musician and you are making music, there is no time to think, "Am I performing well?" or "Does she like this, does she think I am marvelous?" Our true freedom lies in moving with, not against; in completely accepting what is here and not pursuing anything else. We move in harmony with this dance of life. Everything is transitory, empty; there's no need to cling to passing forms.

One of the hardest things to give up is our little security kit, our collection of reasons for our lives. We must have reasons, we think, or our lives won't be secure. We use all kinds of devices, all kinds of reasons: being a mother, a caretaker, a preservationist, a cat lover, a doctor, a lawyer, a merchant, a chief, whatever. But we don't need to have reasons. What is the reason for that rabbit out there on the lawn? Or for the flowers blooming, or the trees? When the survival kit has been forgotten, when "me" has been forgotten, then we can really join in the dance. Then we are really effective as mothers, caretakers, preservationists, whatever, because our action comes from a different place.

Zen is nothing but seeing into our own true nature, and realizing that we have no fixed form. It's clearly realizing the ground of our being and realizing its imperturbability. If we have grasped this in even the most minute degree, everything becomes zazen. That doesn't mean that we dispense with zazen. I feel somewhat dismayed when people tell me they jog instead of practicing zazen, or they read *Zen in the Art of. . . .* There are a million books called Zen in the art of something or other. But nothing takes the place of zazen. Nothing. Zazen extends itself into our lives, and we are one with whatever confronts us.

What we are doing in zazen is having a taste of this One Mind: just plain, pure, clear Being. How do we come to this? Not by thinking about it, not by grabbing it, not by seeking after it; just by doing what the practice asks. What is it doing through us? What is the Buddha-dharma doing through us? If we get out of the way, what does the Buddha-dharma do?

Therefore, during sesshin, we don't talk unless it is absolutely essential. Talking, of course, diverts our concentration, dilutes our experience. We maintain silence, and this quietness extends to how we open doors, how we walk, how we eat, how we do everything: mindfully. And above all, we don't talk in our minds. We don't have little arguments and conversations with ourselves. We don't need to do that here. Everything is taken care of for us. Food is prepared, the zendo is prepared, everything is prepared. Thinking about outside things is not what we come here to do. So we don't engage in vague, rambling discussions.

What is Buddhism about, after all? What are the Three Fundamental Precepts? To do good acts, as much as possible, inconspicuously. To refrain from bad acts, acts that are inappropriate to our lives. And to keep our minds pure and warm. This compassionate activity, this warmth certainly includes abandoning vague discussions. When we really realize, truly understand, that thinking cannot give birth to the essence of thought, that we can never understand this matter by thinking—when our minds are truly silent—then clear, alive, dynamic, wide-awake, vividly present mind flourishes.

Vimilakirti was a layperson, like so many of us, yet he was extraordinary, and people were often afraid to go and see him, because they feared they could never have anything sufficiently significant to bring to him. One day, however, Manjusri summoned up all his courage and went to see Vimilakirti. He asked him, "What is the doctrine of nonduality as realized by a bodhisattva?" Vimilakirti asked him the same question in turn. Manjusri replied, "As I understand it, the doctrine is realized when one looks upon all things as beyond every form of expression and demonstration and as transcending knowledge and argument. This is my comprehension. May I ask you what your understanding is?" Vimilakirti sat with a thunderous silence.

All our teachers, Dogen Zenji, Rinzai Zenji, all these wonderful teachers of ours, are all saying the same thing to us. Turn the light on and return to the source where we always have been. How do we do this? We maintain our thunderous silence, letting go of all words and thoughts, all grasping, all rejection; not holding on to any experience, whether wonderful or awful. We let it go. We are here to wake up to what we have been from the very beginning.

Do not compare. This day is like no other day. This sesshin is like no other sesshin. Just become very plain, ordinary, simple. You have nothing to do. Nothing to do. *You* get out of the way. Shunryu Suzuki Roshi said, "When you say, 'I breathe,' that 'I' is extra." Same thing: It has nothing to do with you. You get out of the way. When you think you have a practice, and you have to do thus and so, what you have is a big impediment. Right away, the mind is set in opposition. Right away, you have duality.

By the third day of sesshin, your mind may be in pretty good condition: quite quiet, quite clear. But now some of you come to the interview room and say, "I want to do better. I want to become more quiet, I want to become more clear. I want to succeed at this."

Better get rid of that right away. Give it up. Please have no thought of improving your condition; no thought about whether it is good or bad—yesterday was terrible, this morning was pretty clear, this afternoon is going to be great—no thoughts like these at all, please.

When you come to see me in the interview room, we *do* speak together about what your condition is, what is happening, of course. And we work together to try to help you clarify things a little more, usually with some attention to your breathing, your posture, some attitude that can perhaps be turned around. But please, while you are sitting do not give one thought to this notion of improving your zazen. Just sit.

If we don't make these distinctions, if we do not get involved in holding on to these ups and downs, but just let them exist, like our in-breaths and out-breaths, then we may have a taste of something.

We come to sesshin and we want to clean up our lives, and some of us have ideas about becoming enlightened in a few short days. But in seeking to become one with Buddha there is separation. We are enlightened from the very beginning. Believe this. We are all enlightened from the very beginning. Have faith in this, and your practice will go all by itself. Have faith in this Buddha-mind.

There are many stories about how Zen masters have dealt with this matter. One student came and said to his teacher, "I want to become a Buddha." The teacher said, "There is no Buddha," breaking this attachment to striving for something, for an end.

Another student went to his teacher and said, "I want to

practice to attain the Way." The teacher replied, "There is no Way to be attained by practice."

Still another student told his teacher, "I want to attain liberation." The teacher said, "Who is holding you back?"

And a student who was full of very flowery thoughts—which I hear quite often in my interview room—said, "I have heard it said that Shakyamuni Buddha left home, practiced for many years, and attained enlightenment." His teacher replied, "Ha! What a pity. If I had seen that old Buddha, I would have given him a good beating and thrown him to the dogs."

These statements are not hurting Buddha or Buddhism. They are not irreverent, not disrespectful. They are made to remove the slightest attachment in the student's mind. A mind free of discrimination is free to practice. Then there is no separation between you and Buddha; no separation between you and liberation.

This practice of ours is to be in tune with the natural way, so that our true nature can show itself. Just to practice according to the teaching given us by Buddha, and not to think about whether we are successful or not—that is our way.

Someone came to me and said in disbelief, "This is spiritual practice, sitting on a cushion and counting from one to ten?"

Everything is spiritual practice. When you leave the zendo, you go back to all kinds of life situations; you are not taking anything with you. You are going back with nothing. Not a thing. You are going back, however, to respond to whatever your life situation is, vividly. This is what our practice is about. Some people are doing koan study. It's not what you say to me in your response, it's *how* you respond. And how do you respond to your life? Don't take anything with you. Then there's just this cleared-up mind that responds to whatever is asked of you.

Those of you who are doing this strange spiritual practice of counting your breaths are discovering that it's exceedingly wonderful; it is incomparably the best way to take us into the ocean of *samadhi* (one-pointed concentration). Just counting: it's difficult to do, to count from one to ten, again and again. To reach a unified, single-minded state, this method has been used for generation after generation after generation. When you begin counting, there are many thoughts. Thoughts come in and thoughts go out, and eventually, the counting takes over and you are deeply engaged in vast—what? And then, just naturally, counting stops. And you're just watching the breath, breathing the in-breath, breathing the out-breath. And then even that falls off, and you're just purely being. The thought of practicing Zen is gone. The thought of successful practice is gone. Scattered mind is gone. There's just simply one-mindedness, and then no-mindedness: *Mu-shin.* Nothing seeking, or striving, or getting; just counting. Just breathing. Just being. Just *this.*

Whatever else we do—and we may very well do all kinds of things besides counting our breaths as our practice goes on—the best way to begin each sitting is just this way. A dynamically still process, a simple, unaffected trust is what occurs.

Last night I was dreaming; it was a very vivid dream. I woke myself up saying, "Yes, yes, yes. Oh, yes, yes, yes!" Say yes to it. Neither approving nor rejecting, whatever it is. Through the intensive practice of sesshin, we can face things more calmly. With our hearts full of strength and energy, we have a new sureness in our lives. We feel lifted out of the ego-self that says "I, me, my, I, me, my" all the time. We feel freer to live in wholeness, not some split, childish self.

This is what we mean by compassion. Being really present with everything, giving ourselves up completely, is compassion. Doing our work as we are asked to do it cleanly, quietly, inconspicuously, is compassion. The two great underpinnings of Buddhism are karuna and prajna, compassion and wisdom. Prajna without karuna is cold. We must be careful that in our Zen practice, in our searching for wisdom, we do not overlook the other side. Compassion without wisdom may result in sentimentality, something that is too soft, too mushy, something that needs more backbone. Traditionally, on the altar in the zendo in Zen temples are two figures on either side of the main image of Buddha or Bodhidharma: one is Samantabhadra, the other Manjusri. Samantabhadra, the bodhisattva of compassion, is riding on an elephant; Manjusri, the bodhisattva of wisdom, is on a lion. Keeping this balance of wisdom and compassion is everyone's koan. When is it appropriate to offer, when to hold back?

With our ordinary minds, we carry out the subtle action of inaction. Returning to whatever our life's work is: getting up in the morning, putting on our clothes, washing our face, going to work, coming back from work, walking downstairs. All of these are wonderful acts of inaction when we do them freely, flowingly, not self-consciously. When we become self-conscious and are separated from the action we are engaged in, we become stiff, unnatural; our minds get twisted up. When we are just walking, just sitting, just going to work, just washing, it's one treasure, one act.

The Bodhisattva Kannon grows arms and heads in abundance to be able to respond wherever there is a need. This bodhisattva spirit in each of us bows down in humble gratitude as we become freer, more awake and aware of what it means to be a true friend. Nobody is forcing us to do something; we spontaneously do what needs to be done. This one treasure is found within ourselves. This untaught wisdom is found in all the subtle actions of our lives.

8

Close Attention

MY DEAR FRIEND Ed Brown says he calls the fourth day of sesshin "limp day." By the fourth day, we have discovered our limp. We realize we can't breeze through untouched, unscathed. Where is our limp? Are we hiding it?

A monk asked Tozan, "Cold and heat descend upon us. How can we avoid them?" Sickness, disappointment, all kinds of things descend upon us. How do we get through these things? Tozan told the monk, "Why don't you go where there is no cold or heat?" Why don't we go where there is no sickness, no disappointment? Where is that place of no cold, no heat, no sickness, no disappointment?

Tozan himself had studied with many important masters, including Nansen, Isan, and Ungan. He worked for a long time with Chu Kokushi's "sermons by insentient creatures." He begged Isan, "Please explain. Why can't I understand it?" Isan sent him to Ungan. When he asked Ungan, "Who can hear the sermons of insentient creatures?", Ungan raised his whisk (just as Isan had done) and asked, "Do you hear?" Tozan still didn't get it. Then Ungan said, "Don't you know the sutra says, 'Birds and trees all meditate on the Buddha and the Dharma'?" Tozan suddenly understood. He continued his practice, training, training, and training, doing zazen with close attention. This close, ever-watchful attention brought him to a great realization: one day, when he was wading across a stream, he looked in the water and saw his reflection, and he experienced something quite wonderful.

Like Tozan, we are often asking, "Please explain. I don't understand what Zen is all about." What about this Zen training? It's not like any other religious or philosophical training. We don't go to theological seminary and sit down and study a long list of books. What is our training? It is endless. There is no end to it. In becoming a priest, we don't just get a certificate saying we have answered all sorts of questions and are now ready to do what we are supposed to do. This is a life-long training. It is life itself. Yes, we come together for sesshin every month, and some of us are here in the zendo almost all the time, and this makes for wonderful training. That is one side of it. The other side is that we must sit alone, work alone, and live our life in this fundamental solitude. We come together for inspiration, for refreshment from one another in this endless training.

When I was ordained, my teacher said, "Now you must realize that you have to train harder than anyone else. You have to sit more, you have to attend more sesshin, you have to study harder. Do you realize what you have taken on? Endless, life-long, life-after-life-long training."

When Tozan was enlightened, he said, "Understanding this Way, I can be as I am." Can we be as we are? Stripped down to zero? Just plain, ordinary, simple, with no pretension? This zero is emptiness, no content. The idea of zero comes from India. Buddha understood it very well, and he tried to convey to his disciples, to us, this understanding. Zero exists because of the activity of emptiness. We experience this activity as impermanence. Everything changes. There is no end to it. Moment after moment, breath after breath, everything is constantly changing. And at the same time, we discover that which never changes.

This Buddha-nature, or Tao, or absolute ground of our being—this never changes, and it is from this that form derives.

A flower blooms; the petals fall; it dies. Birds come. They sing; they fly away. Rocks in the garden are quietly disintegrating. Everywhere, there is birth, growth, death, decay. Every moment, without ceasing even for a second, there is being, nonbeing, the activity of impermanence. Every day we chant in the *Heart Sutra,* "Form is emptiness, emptiness is form." This is the function of impermanence. But just thinking about this, just using our discriminating mind, our small-self mind, we cannot understand. We must come to the place before that discriminating mind was born, where there are no names, where there is no "is it or isn't it," where there is no cold, no heat. This is the place we come to in deep zazen. This condition is known as the samadhi of no conflict. There is no argument that remains; no discriminating self; no self and other. We experience everyone and everything as Self.

"Where is the place where there is no cold or heat?" the monk asked Tozan. He replied, "When cold, let it be so cold that it kills you; when hot, let it be so hot that it kills you." When in a hot place, become one with the heat. When in a cold place, be one with the coldness. Don't resist, whatever it is. When cold, shiver. When hot, sweat.

There is a story about Kanro, a fast dog that chased a rabbit. They both ran so fast that they fell down dead of exhaustion. The monk is running after the problem of life and death. Run, run, run; ask, ask, ask. When we finally enter "the ancient emerald palace," a poetic expression for the samadhi of no discrimination, what do we find? Zero.

9

Depending on Nothing

ON APRIL 8, Buddha's birthday, we celebrated with fifteen so-called children and thirty other children of older ages and stages. I told the story of Buddha Shakyamuni being born a prince in a little state in India. When his mother, Lady Maya, was nearing the time when she was ready to give birth, she wanted to return to her native place, and on the way she stopped at a garden full of flowers. When she raised her arm to pick one of these flowers from a tree, the Buddha was born. He immediately stood up, the story goes, and took seven steps eastward, then seven steps westward, then south, and then north, seven steps. Then at the center he stopped. Raising his right hand, and pointing with his left hand to the earth, he proclaimed: "Above the heavens and beneath the earth, I am the noblest one."

Of course a newborn baby cannot walk seven steps in any direction. But this has a special meaning. "Above the heavens, beneath the earth, I am the noblest one." It's the same for every one of us. Everyone is the noblest one. You, I, and everything in the universe; here, there, everything is nothing but the noblest one.

Here's another story, one that takes place in our time. When

Soen Nakagawa Roshi came to the United States for the first time, it was on Buddha's birthday. At his first Zen meeting in San Francisco, someone gave him a baby Buddha statue as a gift to welcome him to America. While he was here he kept that baby Buddha with him. During his morning service he bowed to that baby Buddha, chanted with that baby Buddha. On his way home to Japan, after sitting quietly on the deck of the ship one morning, he threw the baby Buddha into the ocean. So that baby Buddha is now standing at the bottom of the Pacific Ocean, proclaiming, "Above the heavens, beneath the earth, even at the bottom of the Pacific Ocean, there is nothing else but the noblest one."

Once a monk came to Joshu, and quoted a famous saying by Sosan, the Third Patriarch: "The Great Way has no difficulties—just avoid choice and attachment." And then he asked Joshu, "What are nonchoice and nonattachment?" Joshu answered, "Throughout heaven and earth, I alone am the noblest one." Each one of us alone is the noblest one throughout heaven and earth. From the beginning there is nothing dualistic. It is beyond asking "Is it or isn't it?" The monk who was asking Joshu this question was still caught in a relative point of view: choice and attachment or nonchoice and nonattachment.

The sun shines, the moon shines, the rain rains. They shine and rain on all of us. They do not exclude anyone. When clouds come, what? Cloudiness. When rains come? Raininess. As Ummon said with stunning simplicity, "Every day is a good day." It is when our discriminating minds interfere that we have trouble.

We tend to see everything outside ourselves through the conceptualizing of color, shape, sound, taste, touch, and so on. But do we truly see? Do we truly taste the essence? When we *think* of something as good or bad it is due to our own habit of thought. It is because we have so much attachment to this discriminating mind that we do not experience our Buddha-nature, or absolute consciousness, or whatever we may call it.

With our zazen, we are learning to give up this imagined individual self. We are melting it into *Muuuuu*. With one long, deep, wonderful breath, melting down, melting down.

Some kind person came and asked me, "How are you feeling in this springtime all alone?"*Depending on nothing, how do I feel at sixty-five in the springtime, alone? I said, "Good! Really good! Inside there is still a sixteen-year-old girl, happy no matter what." And that is because of this wonderful practice, in which we are always refreshed, always renewed, always coming to realize that there *is* This Mind that is never disturbed. So often we do depend on this or that, instead of having our own experience; we depend on thoughts that have been thought by someone else. What is it like to depend on ourselves alone, on our own experience? We come to understand that we are a part of the whole universe, not some separate self. We do not understand this by reading about it, but through our own digging into ourselves. "Before you have penetrated, it all seems like a silver mountain, like an iron wall," Engo says. "When you have been able to penetrate, from the beginning it was your self that was the silver mountain, the iron wall." Buddha-nature is everywhere. When our minds are clear as crystal, all the Dharma is revealed: here, there, inside, outside, visible, invisible.

Some people think that Zen Buddhism has just arrived here and that they have to propagate the faith, so to speak. This is nonsense. Zen Buddhism has been here a long, long time, quietly doing its work. Calmly and peacefully, people have been practicing for years and years and years. We have a beautiful temple, a beautiful house dedicated to this noble religion. But a Buddhist temple has nothing to do with bricks and stones. Such a temple is built of pure, eager, willing, and loving hearts. There is nothing mysterious in Buddhism, and there is no propagation, no compulsion. No one is going to bind anyone's will. But

---

*Maurine had recently separated from her husband of many years, Ozzie Freedgood.

within the strong, formal practice that we are engaged in, we find our own freedom. This is a place where all of us, from all walks of life, with various levels of education, points of view, and backgrounds, have come together to help one another in a true bodhisattva spirit. We chant the Four Great Vows together: I vow to save all sentient beings. I vow to get rid of my delusions. I vow to master the Way. I vow to follow the Path. Endlessly. We are not here for tranquilization or some sort of pleasant effect, but for something much deeper. We are here to practice together, deeply and clearly, and to live it without saying one word about it. We certainly are not doing this in order to be able to say, "My life is so much better since I started doing Zen practice." Nonsense. So it is, but there is no need to say so.

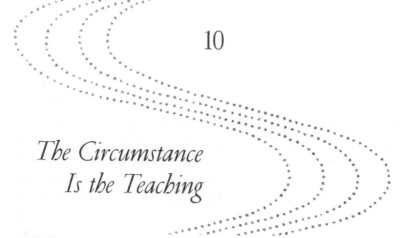

10

The Circumstance Is the Teaching

PEOPLE SOMETIMES ask me, "Did you have to pass examinations and study a lot to become a priest?" Lived experience is what we need to be priests and teachers. To study the sutras and to know the history of our tradition is fine, but it is only our own lived experience that we can use and give away to someone else.

There was once a monk named Isan, who studied all the Theravada and Mahayana texts, but this didn't seem to make him feel more at ease; in fact, he felt dis-ease. His mind was wobbly. So he went to Master Hyakujo's place, and sat down on a cushion, and sat, and sat, and sat, and after some time he became Hyakujo's attendant monk. One evening, while he was sitting, Hyakujo suddenly said, "Who are you?" The monk, surprised, told him his name. "Go and look in the fire," Hyakujo said. "See if any burning embers remain." So he went over to the fire and dug around, dug around, and couldn't find anything. There were just ashes. It was just as his sitting had been—cold ashes. The teacher came over, and dug around with the tongs. Deep in the ashes, he found one tiny ember. He held it out. And Isan was enlightened. He suddenly realized that deep down inside himself was this living fire.

Deep inside each one of us is this living ember. We must dig down, deeper and deeper, unafraid of what we will find there. This zazen is not just something to make us happy; that's not enough. We go deeper, deeper. Where is that wonderful living coal? So we sit, quietly, intensely, gratefully, joyfully— experiencing for ourselves the living aspects of our sitting.

Some Zen texts refer to the condition in which the mind is like an incense burner in which everything has burned down, burned out. That is a true description, and yet it seems to conflict with this story about the living ember. But please remember that we can never express the essence of Zen with words. We find all kinds of contradictory statements. We can't say Zen is this or that. We must enact it; we must show it through a spontaneous, lively, spirited act. At the same time, Zen is not showing off with wild, eccentric behavior. The action of the moment comes out of long, disciplined practice, and is used to demonstrate the essential teaching without saying one word.

Some time after the above encounter with Hyakujo, Isan showed his understanding through such an act. Among Hyakujo's disciples was a man who was a fortune-teller, basing his predictions upon physiognomy or the aspect of a house or site. One day he came to Hyakujo and said, "I have found a good place to build a monastery. The spirits of the mountain indicate that it has the power to attract fifteen hundred monks." But, he added, Hyakujo was not to go there himself. "This mountain is round, and you are too thin. If you are there, with your poor physique, only one thousand monks will come; let's try for the maximum number!"

Hyakujo called the monks together so that the fortune-teller could appraise their suitability. The head monk, who thought he would surely be the one, was rejected immediately. Next came Isan, who at the time was working as the *tenzo,* the person in charge of meals. Instantly, the fortune-teller chose him. And so Hyakujo gave him Dharma transmission, and asked him to establish the new monastery. The head monk, who had an enormous ego, was very angry, and demanded another test. So a public examination was held. Hyakujo assembled the monks once again, and set a water bottle on the floor. "You may not call this a water jug," he told them. "What will you call it?" The head monk's reply was, "It cannot be called a stump." Then Isan was asked for his response, and he immediately kicked it over. He did this with no intention of passing this test, with no conception of whether it would be seen as a good or bad action, he simply responded freely, openly, as if to say, "I'm busy in the kitchen. Let me get back to work."

After he became head of the new monastery, Isan didn't hang a sign out announcing the sitting schedule or public lectures. He just sat, and gradually, people came. Sure enough, eventually fifteen hundred monks assembled. Somehow or other, word gets around about what's going on. I have never advertised our activities at the Cambridge Buddhist Association, and it's hard to find us. The sign on our door is about the size of a postage stamp. Yet somehow people find their way here. When we first acquired the building, I sat by myself, day after day after day. Soon other people came. We put together a sitting schedule according to the times they were arriving. Then we started doing sesshin, and here we are.

Isan took off his cook's headband and put on the yoke of the teacher. It's hard work to be the head of the monastery. It requires constant vigilance. There is no way we can back off, or say, "I can't do this." *I* can't do it; the Dharma has asked that it be done. So we're here.

Everything is our teacher, and is reminding us of the teachings. All the circumstances of our life are teaching us. The real sermon, the real preaching is when people act in ways that are appropriate to the circumstances of their lives. Each one of us has a profound teaching given to us. Sometimes it is illness, sometimes death.

Yesterday a woman came and told me about the suicide of her father. It was a terrible shock. She had made every effort to make him well: had engaged the finest doctors, the best psychiatrists in the country, the best medicine, the most renowned hospitals, everything. So why did he kill himself? What a teaching that was! He chose, he told her over and over again, not to live. He wanted to give it up. But she kept forcing her own idea on him, that it was better to live. Who knows whether it is better for someone else to live or to die? How do we learn to accept this; how do we learn not to force our egocentric ideas on others, even when we think they are not mentally competent?

We are all given such Zen tests, day by day. What is our test? What is our day-by-day koan? It has nothing to do with searching in books for answers, but with responding as Isan did, creatively and freely. Our responses must come out of our own Zen spirit, not out of some foolish imitation of what we think a spontaneous act would be. Self-consciously unusual or eccentric behavior merely stinks of Zen. With strong, disciplined practice, we discover the emptiness out of which comes true freedom, true creativity.

11

Building a Temple

THE BUDDHA, while out walking one day, stopped and
pointed and said, "This is a wonderful spot to build a temple." A bodhisattva stepped forward, placed a flower on that
spot, and said, "I have just built a beautiful temple."

Certain places are considered especially good sites for building a temple. Friends in Kentucky bought a piece of land they
felt would be a great spot for Buddhist practice. Other friends,
Tibetan Buddhist practitioners, found a fine site in Nova Scotia.
The top of this house in Syracuse is a wonderful place to have a
temple.

But where is the most wonderful spot to build a temple? It is
in each one of us. The bodhisattva placing a flower on that spot
is a bodhisattva placing a flower in our hearts. Each one of us,
sitting on our cushions, is building a beautiful temple. Wherever
we are is a wonderful place to build a temple.

Someone came to me and said, "I feel I'm so lacking." At this
moment, what do you lack? Not a thing. "As the truth eternally
reveals itself, this very place is the lotus land of purity; this very
body is the body of the Buddha," Hakuin said. This very spot is
a wonderful place to build a temple.

In the beginning of our practice we feel we have to do so much. We conceptualize about what we find in the many books we read: "Am I having that experience, should I be doing this or that, is that what it's all about?" Books are important, and can inspire us to sit more deeply and have some clearer understanding. But when we are sitting in zazen, we don't ponder what we have read. We just let the mind rest in its natural state, and have our own experience of something wonderful. If we trust this mind in ourselves, at this moment, what do we lack? Can we give up the small, egocentric, grabby self? Can we let this mind take care of it?

The essence of our practice is letting the ego-self fall away, melt down. It is the practice of forgetting the self. As we become less self-conscious, we become more open and more warmly present, and what we discover as this melting down takes place is that what we really are is the pure, clear, lighted mind itself— nothing else. So the aimless aim, the goalless goal of our zazen is to conduct our lives from this clear, lighted mind, this always just-beginning mind.

When he was about ninety years of age, Dr. D. T. Suzuki said that he was just beginning to understand Zen, just having some inkling of what comes from this ever-beginning mind. True insight is always just out of reach. It's endless. If there were a finish line, if we had some experience and that was all there was to it, what a pity. It's just beginning. Having some little opening of our inner eye, we then go on and on and *on!* Not yet, not yet. This Zen insight is not *our* awareness, but Buddha-mind's awareness of itself in us. This Buddha-mind, this awareness, is out of time, out of space; it is not subject to circumstances, and has no name.

Someone said to me, "Why do Mu? Why not just breathe?" It's the same! There is no name; it's just Mu-shin, which can be translated as "no-mind." People who haven't experienced zazen may hear the term "no-mind" and say, "What is this 'no-mind'?

When you meditate, you're not supposed to think, so your brain must go blank, right?"

Of course we think. We can never get rid of thoughts completely, and to imagine that we can is unrealistic. So to judge ourselves, to chastise ourselves for our thoughts is a waste of time. But how do we deal with this thinking? Thinking is pondering, considering, weighing, judging, and so on; having an argument back and forth in our minds. Not thinking is the denial of thinking, denying what is going on in spite of ourselves. Zazen is something else. Zazen is completely accepting the presence of ideas, of thoughts, without either affirming or denying them, without engaging them. Sometimes there is a life situation to which we must direct our attention. At such a time, of course we must think it through. We think it down to the last drop, but we do not fool ourselves that we are practicing zazen.

Thoughts are not our enemies in zazen. Our thoughts are endless, inexhaustible. This is the nature of our minds. Thoughts are not bad. We let them come, but we do not pursue them. What do we do with this powerful energy that comes about through our sitting? Instead of using it to engage in these thoughts, to make arguments in our mind, "to raise waves where there is no wind," what do we do? We have excellent practices to help us: counting our breaths, just counting them. Chanting inwardly, just chanting. Staying with the koan, becoming the koan. Being Mu, nothing but Mu. Just inhaling, just exhaling, the breath just as it is, without getting tense, without judging, weighing, or considering. Just this.

There is a difference between not thinking and being without thinking. The difference is between a simple negation and the Buddhist doctrine of emptiness, *sunyata*. The Buddhist doctrine of sunyata is the pure presence of things just as they are, without thinking, with no intentional attitude at all. No "I believe this to be the case," no "Is it or isn't it." Pure presence. This reaches the ground of our being, our clear, pure mind, and then we have a base for our thinking and reflection. That's what our practice is for. What does it give us for our lives? A strong seat; a firm base. Then life can be dealt with, hara full, heart full, head cool.

Our thoughts and illusions are not in the fundamental nature of our minds. They are temporary; they come and go. We can let go of them. We become much more healthy minded through realizing that we are not stuck in some fixed condition. We all may have periods of weariness, or pain, but it's just a passing, impermanent condition. And fundamentally we are all Buddha from the very beginning.

12

Taking It Home

PEOPLE COME to Zen practice for various reasons. Those who come due to suffering are the most numerous. Many come because they have big questions about life. Some come just out of curiosity. Some think they come to study Buddhism. And what is it to study Buddhism?

Dogen Zenji said: "To study Buddhism is to study the self. To study the self is to forget the self. To forget the self is to perceive oneself in all beings, in all things." And the essence of our practice is just this. We come because there is something inside that we want to find out about; we have glimmers of it, little tastes of it, and we think, Ah! What is this? And as we find out about it, we let go of the impediment of the small ego-self; we become less self-conscious, less worried about how we are doing, more present, and we open up to the realization that we are in all things. Not just good things, wonderful things, great things, beautiful things, but everything. And we accept it all, open to it all. A pure, clear, lighted mind is what we have discovered.

What teaches us this? Our own zazen, our own practice. Teachers can encourage us, listen to us, hit us when the occasion calls for it, straighten our posture, suggest things that might be helpful, but it is our practice that really teaches us, moment after moment.

Some people come to Sparks Street and say, "I want to study Zen." What does it mean to study Zen? We often hear, "Where can I enter the way of Zen? How can I study Zen?" When a student asked this of the Zen master Kyosei, the master asked a question in turn: "What is the noise outside?" "That is the voice of the raindrops," the student said. "Enter from there," Kyosei replied.

Right now, enter from wherever you are. It's all open, an open secret. Enter from listening to the birds. Enter from feeling the sunlight in this room. There are any number of wonderful ways to study Zen. There are lots of books about Zen, and some of them are helpful. Some of them are an impediment. What is most important is how you feel it yourself. How does this transform your life? How deeply are you willing to go into the roots of your Self? How willing are you to really know who you are? Many of us are afraid to do that. We just take the soft, pallid approach: "Oh, this makes me feel good. Ah yes, I feel better now." Sometimes I want to say, "I'm sorry about that." I wish you felt something so deeply that then, eventually, you'd have true peace of mind. Then, no matter what comes, it won't knock you about.

If your attitude is soft and mushy, it's no good. This is not studying Zen. This is taking a tranquilizer. To study Zen requires enormous patience. I think often about my friend Lydia Bobritsky, who was about eighty-two or eighty-three when I last saw her, and was still studying Zen, and still having deep and wonderful experiences. When I visited her, I asked, "What is your practice now?"

"I am studying how to die," she said. Then I asked her, "How did you come to your wonderful condition of enlightenment?" And she said, "I concentrate on one thing at a time and I count my breaths. That's it." One act, one place. This is what we are here to experience. This is what we come to really know in our body and mind. Our whole history is in our body. So, no daydreaming, please, about things that are not possible; no imagining things that don't exist. Be one with heaven and earth. Nothing else. It's very easy to say and not so easy to do, I know. But let us try. Let us open ourselves up.

There are always grieving people among us; always some who are having a very difficult time. A practice that has helped me enormously in difficult times, and still does, is to chant. Inwardly chanting, chanting, chanting, chanting. Chanting the *Heart Sutra,* chanting the *Kannon Sutra,* chanting *Namu dai bosa.* When the mind becomes very unruly and loud and angry and nervous, chant, chant, chant. At every opportunity, chant. What is the scenery in your mind today? Namu dai bosa, Namu dai bosa, Namu dai bosa, Namu dai bosa—to unite with boundless bodhisattvahood, with the ground of our being, for the sake of all beings.

And listening, listening practice. What is the noise outside? What is the sound in the house? What do we really hear? Do we resist the sound and say, "This is disturbing me, I can't concentrate because there is this noise or that noise," or do we simply become one with it? To become one with chanting, one with listening, takes us out of ourselves, out of all this fussy stuff, the endless numbers of things that get in the way. It extends our minds. It broadens our consciousness. Those are pretty pretentious phrases. Forgive me, but you know what I mean. We become one with the listening, one with the chanting. And there is no thought of doing well or not doing well.

Somebody comes to dokusan and says to me, "I think I'm making progress with my zazen." Oh, really? How do you know that? You have to be out of it to know that. If you are right in it, you have no thought, no feeling of doing well or badly. You and it are one. When you get up from sitting, you may feel some wonderful effect, but while you are doing it, please don't judge it. Or I should rather say, when it is doing you, don't judge it. "My zazen is going well." Nonsense.

In the *Surangama Sutra,* the Buddha instructs us to enter samadhi, this deep, concentrated state of mind, from listening—starting with listening, being one with listening. Thich Nhat Hanh asks his students just to listen to the sound of the gong. Every so often he stops talking and just does this. (Gong is struck.) When we strike this gong we should let it sing down to its bottom drop, like this. It takes our zazen right down if our mind is with that sound, the whole body and mind with that sound. It's a most wonderful way to enter samadhi. So those of you who strike the gong, take your time. Don't go (gong is rung three times in quick succession). No good. It sounds like a fire alarm. (Gong is rung once.) One clear sound. One pure, clear sound. No thoughts about whether that sound is soft or that sound is harsh or why didn't I strike this gong better or whatever. Just do it! Just listen. Just be here with the sound.

Sitting here in this beautiful house, we have an idyllic condition. It couldn't be better. It's not too hot, not too cold; we have wonderful food, a clean house, kind people—it's idyllic. But when you go home, what happens? Someone who has to leave today asked me, "What do I do when I go home? How do I carry this with me? How do I nourish it every day, and how do I not lose it in all the busy round of activities that I have to be engaged in?"

This person might come and say to me this afternoon, "Why don't you enlighten me before I go home? Hurry up!" Since you are enlightened from the very beginning, there is nothing for me to do. And it is your life's work to wake up to the fact that you are enlightened from the beginning. So for me to do anything is redundant, superfluous, and downright intrusive. When the mind is at rest in one deed, one word, we can lead a singular, simple life even in the midst of many different activities and many different places. This is the everyday life practice that you take home with you. Whatever you are doing from morning until evening, your mind has not shifted from its simple and direct quality. Your mind and body are one! This is your temple. This is your zendo where you practice, and this you take with you everywhere. If you simply see yourself in your own temple in your own everyday life, without any pretense; without fibbing to yourself about why you are doing things or what your grand motives are; if you are just clearly and plainly doing what you are doing, then you can be clear with other people.

This house, when I first saw it, was full of furniture. This room had every single space, from floor to ceiling, covered with something: furniture, paintings, rugs. But it has become a wonderful Buddhist temple. Someone who had grown up in this house came to visit us, and walked around, and then said appreciatively, "It's so different. But it's very nice."

So this old New England house is a temple. We don't have any Oriental eaves, but the important quality is here. The bodhisattva who put a flower down and proclaimed that he had just built a wonderful temple is each one of us. We come and put ourselves down, we straighten up our spines, fill our bodies full of energy, and see what happens. Flower mind is what happens. We begin opening up, discovering this beautiful, blooming mind. Heart and hara open in full bloom, showing each one of us the place where a beautiful temple is being built.

When someone comes to me and says, "It's all very well sitting here, but how do I take this into my life?" my answer is, You don't. We can't. *It* takes us. *We* don't do it. *It* is present moment after moment, leading us in whatever we are doing. In this condition of Mu-shin—no mind, empty, cleared-up mind—we meet one another in a fundamental way, just clearly presenting ourselves to each other as we are.

When we return home after sesshin and someone asks us what we did, it's better not to say too much. It's best to say nothing. First of all, nobody really understands what we are doing here unless they engage in it themselves; second, if we talk too much about these wonderful experiences, it dilutes them, and pretty soon we're only left with the shadow of something that was really beautiful and deeply meaningful in our inner lives. Sometimes people are just asking out of idle curiosity. Sometimes, if they continue to ask, you sense that they do have some feeling of what is happening to you. But don't just throw it around. It's too precious.

In Buddhism, we speak about the two truths: relative truth and absolute truth. All words, all beliefs, belong to relative truth. All the things that you have read and studied and pondered may be true from a particular point of view at a certain time, but no more than that. Everything changes. Nothing lasts forever—not even these things that we may think are so true. A dogmatic attitude about these matters, about one's beliefs and opinions, is against the true nature of things. It doesn't fit. Sitting on the cushion, we understand this. We come to understand these changes. We are experiencing the subtle changes in our attitude, in our body and its condition, in the way we taste our food, in the way our feet feel the floor, in the way we hear everything. Everything changes. This moment is what we have: nothing else. That's it. So open up to it more and more. No intolerant and self-righteous attitudes, please. Just find out for yourselves, in a calm and reasonable way, what this wonderful practice is about. Let us accept and work with whatever our present condition has brought us. And in doing this, even a hard life can become a joyful one. Sitting on the cushion, we are tuning in to the first principle of the universe, sensing what an amazing and marvelous opportunity this life as a human being is.

13

The Taste of Zen

SPIRITUAL TRANSFORMATION is a rather grand-sounding phrase, but that is what we are engaged in. And hard work it is. There is pain and weariness, there are many doubts and questions. But this is a practice of body and mind coming together. It is not just sitting and thinking, but being dynamically aware, sensing with our entire bodies. We let the breath go into all the places in us that hurt—not just the physical wounds, but all the wounds of our life. The breath enters tenderly, warmly, healingly. Our zazen posture is a posture of healing. It is open and alert; the healing breath moves freely through us.

The word meditation comes from the Latin *meditare,* which is the passive form of the verb, meaning "being moved to the center." It is not the active form, which is "moving to the center." We are being moved to the center. This center is our own essence. Sitting after sitting, letting everything go, we become more aware of our own personal center. We become more rooted in it. This simple act of sitting absolutely still, letting everything drop off, has far-reaching effects.

Sitting still is not what some of us may have imagined spiritual practice to be. We may think that it involves something more impressive. But those of us who do it, those of us who are *present* at this moment, know that this is it. Sitting absolutely still, body and mind are not separate. Our state of mind at any given moment becomes clearer in this condition of being present, completely present. And there is great healing power in this.

Of course we have pain. The true taste of Zen really cannot be understood unless we have some pain. So we do not resist that pain. We invite it in, and we find that it's not so bad. We don't move against it; we don't struggle with it; rather, we simply breathe into it and discover what it can do to change our condition. We see what happens when we pay attention to it.

I often ask students, "Why did you come to sit? What is your reason? Do you have a reason? What happened in your life that brought you to the cushion? Why are you here?" And most people say they came because they wanted to have some peace of mind. As we sit, there is some temporary peacefulness, of course. But we want to come to a condition of mind that takes us through all the circumstances of our life, no matter how difficult. Then, no matter what happens, there is this quiet, truly peaceful space within. And unless we endure some pain, some weariness, we cannot really taste this; without it, our practice may not ever go really deep. Please don't misunderstand. This doesn't mean we should inflict anything on ourselves. It simply means that if pain comes, we let it come, and we let it be our teacher. Thus, even illness can be a wonderful teacher for us.

Pain and joy, samsara and nirvana are not separate. Delusion and enlightenment are not separate. Even the words "separate or together" are not separate. There was a Zen master named Jizo who decided to live alone on a little farm. There he continued his practice, sitting as much as he wanted to, working as much as he wanted to. He lived in a tiny hut, sat, and worked. One day, four traveling monks stopped for a visit. They didn't know who was living there, but they thought they would investigate. Jizo asked them in and he gave them whatever hospitality he could offer. He apologized that his hut was too small to hold all of them, but he built them a nice fire outdoors so that they could sit around it and be comfortable, eat, and relax. When they were finished with their meal and had rested awhile, he inquired, "It appears that you are Zen monks. In your practice, do you consider yourself and this field, this stone, this hut, separate or not separate?"

These monks didn't realize they were talking to a master. They thought this was some old farmer sitting in his hut. One of them, named Shuzan, answered impatiently. "They are separate. Everybody knows that." Jizo held up two fingers and quietly said, "I have read a little about Buddhism, and according to my understanding, the Buddhist teaching is that self and others are not separate." Shuzan hurriedly said, "Oh yes, of course, there is no separation. Of course, everybody knows that between oneself and one's surroundings there is no separation. Quite right, quite right." And again Jizo held up two fingers. "And so one part of your mind is saying there is differentiation. And another part is saying that there is oneness. What about this?" Shuzan laughed nervously and said to his friends, "Let's get out of here." He did not think this ordinary old farmer had anything to teach him.

How often we miss a great opportunity. So many things are teaching us all the time. The words printed on the label of a tea bag can teach us. But too often, we think, "I want a famous, wonderful, illustrious teacher from some great lineage to teach me. I must find such a person."

The monks set off for southern China, where Buddhism was quite popular. On the journey, Shuzan found that he couldn't stop thinking about the question the farmer had asked, and he felt a little guilty that he had just dismissed this old person. "Are things really separate or are they one? What is this split in my mind? What kind of Zen student am I?" As he pondered these questions, he began to practice very sincerely. There was a lot going on around him, but he continued to practice in his own way, just as each of us must do. We are always surrounded by many activities, many books; there are always interesting lectures to go to; but fundamentally, at bottom, we must find out for ourselves.

And then one day he returned to this old farmer, who was no longer in his overalls, but was instead wearing his robes. This time, Jizo asked Shuzan, "Where have you come from?" In so many Zen stories, this question is asked. What is the real question being posed? Where have you come from? What was your face before your parents were born? Who are you? Where are you going? Why are you here?

As most of us would do, Shuzan gave a literal answer: "I have come from the South" Jizo asked, "How is the Buddha-dharma in the South?" Shuzan told him about all the many discussions, the popularity of *mondo* (Zen question-answer dia logues), the flourishing intellectual life there. Jizo was unimpressed. "Is that so? It doesn't seem as good as what we are doing here."

"What do you do here?" Shuzan inquired.

"We cut down trees and cultivate the fields."

What do we do in our zazen? We cut down the forest of our delusions and cultivate the fields of our true nature. Sitting quietly, we are cutting off, digging, cultivating the Buddha fields. This Buddha-dharma is deeply rooted in our ordinary, everyday activities; lofty discussions miss the mark. In this practice, we engage in our life work completely and fully, reaching our essential being and then expressing it, wherever we are. We can never come to a standstill on this path. We are always moving on, letting ourselves be moved on by the Buddha-dharma.

So, how is the Buddha-dharma in Syracuse today? What is our practice right here, right now? It is always different. It is living. Moving. Changing. Always open. No static condition. Simple. Straightforward. Naturally harmonious. And it is a feeling of deep friendliness. This is the Buddha-dharma today in Syracuse in this room: a deep, wonderful connection with one another. We don't need to say a word, but we feel it. We do not need to smile at one another; we feel one another's bodies smiling at one another. But to smile at the Buddha in us, in each other, is not a bad idea. When you are sitting, every so often, smile at the Buddha in us. We do not need to be grim. This is a joyful practice. Coming through pain, coming through weariness, we experience wonderful joy.

These simple, quiet activities—just sitting, just walking, just eating, just cleaning—are helping us to find a vital way of living, a way to face things fearlessly, directly from our essential being. Today, we are looking at everything as if for the first time. We take no fixed positions; we let our opinions fall away. There is no inner voice insisting, "This is the way *I* have to do it." We are willing to find a new way to do it, a new way to look at it, a new way to open up. This is beginner's mind. We are giving ourselves entirely to each moment, just as we are, rooted on our cushions, rooted in the earth. Sitting on our cushions by our own effort, we feel the wonderful support and encouragement of all others present. What an extraordinary practice we have together: "self" and "other" not separate. In-breath. Out-breath. Receiving. Giving. Just this.

14

Sesshin Mind, Universal Mind

IT IS THE ILLUSION of having some separate self that keeps us from finding inner peace. When we gather together for sesshin, what we are doing is melting down this illusion of a separate self; melting down this idea that there is something to be pacified.

What does the word sesshin mean? The first character, "setsu," means to join, to collect, to receive, to transmit, to continue. And "shin," of course, means mind. We are not here just to collect our minds. This is not just a time for us to receive something, to continue something, to transmit something just for us; it is a time for us to join our minds to the mind of the universe. We are expanding into and realizing this unity of mind with the whole universe.

Sesshin also means fasting—becoming poor in spirit—letting go of everything. Not grasping, not panting after anything, just doing what needs to be done, step by step. Our zazen during sesshin gets stronger, clearer, more alive, more dynamic every day, if we let go of our gaining ideas, our judgmental attitudes about whether or not we are doing well. When I see that you need a little massage, a spinal pickup, I come and do that for you. But the rest is up to you. This is our practice. Zen is not some cold, austere, held-back kind of practice. It is full of warmth, full of a loving nature, full of giving to the whole universe. In everything we do, we affect every other being.

The conscious mind that we use habitually in everyday life becomes unstable from time to time. We all know this. And unless we have time to connect with this universal mind, our condition doesn't improve. When we take this time, when we immerse ourselves in sesshin after sesshin, we find that we are functioning more surely, more clearly, more joyfully, more energetically in our daily life; and above all, we have a better connection with all human beings with whom we come in contact.

When we first start sesshin, we may be very annoyed by something or by somebody's particular way of being. As the days go on, these likes and dislikes melt down, and by the end of five or seven days, there is no more of that judgmental attitude. We have made a deep connection, which has nothing to do with "Is it good? Is it bad? Do I like it? Don't I like it?" It goes far beyond that. This is what we taste together here in sesshin. We get rid of the self-centered mind, the competitive mind, the proud mind, the gaining or losing mind. We let go of all of it.

During these days, we become really aware of how much we are not being true to ourselves, of what we are carrying around with us, of how much unessential stuff we are holding onto so tightly. This practice of fearlessly being who we are—precisely the person we naturally are, with no affectation, no pretension—requires a lot of integrity and a lot of humility. If we are true to ourselves in the depths of our being, then we can be true to all other beings.

Without any self-conscious effort, we just respond spontaneously to what needs to be done. Every time we think we have achieved something, or that we have understood something, or that we know what all of this means, we just throw it away. During this time together, we are constantly paring down, continually letting go of these opinions, these fixed thoughts for or against. And we are committing ourselves to listening, to accepting whatever comes along, rather than closing up or defending ourselves against it. We are participating in a sesshin bath: giving up, letting go, feeling the clarity of what is purifying our minds.

Every day we chant the *Heart Sutra,* which in Sanskrit is called the *Mahaprajnaparamita Sutra,* and in Japanese the *Hannyashingyo.* This *Heart Sutra* is the heart of the matter. The eternal, sacred deed, the endless practice, this is the "gyo" that we do. "Maha" means great, all inclusive, nothing left out. "Prajna" is intuitive wisdom. Everything is sensed with our intuitive wisdom, not just thought out in our heads. "Gone, gone, gone to the other shore" is "paramita." What does this mean? Not going to some other place, but finding nirvana in this very place; having a change of heart; seeing things from a cleared-up, fresh perspective.

What is the Way? The real Way is not difficult. Sosan, Joshu, Nansen, Dogen, Rinzai—all say the same thing in different words. The real Way is not difficult if we avoid choice and attachment, if we don't try to hold on to things or to fix things into some pattern of our own choosing. We are all seeking true peace of mind. But there are no sidetracks, no quick exits, no solutions from the outside. We cannot sit on the cushion and blame our problems on other people, or on society. We have to take full responsibility sitting here.

In so many koans, monks come to the teachers and ask about the Way. What is the Way? Shall I search after it? Shall I work hard to get it? Then will I grasp it? If we try to grasp it, we lose it. If we try to say what it is, it is gone. Our need for security binds us, and causes us to seek some definition for what Zen is. But this mysterious, unspeakable, indefinable something that we are all experiencing together here cannot be put into a mold.

A professor once came to see Nyogen Senzaki at one of his

"floating zendos,"* ready to write down everything he could about Zen. Nyogen Senzaki took him to the zendo, and the man, with his pen and paper ready, started to talk about Zen. Senzaki put his fingers to his lips and said, "Shhh, we meditate in silence here." Then he took him into the kitchen, and the professor thought, "Oh, good, now I can talk. Now let's see what they eat in this place." And he began to ask about that. Senzaki said, "Shhh, we prepare food and eat in silence here." Next, they went to the library, and the professor thought, "Oh, all these wonderful books! Surely we can talk now." But Senzaki said, "We read in silence here." As he showed him to the door, the man was still gasping, "But what is Zen?"†

During sesshin, we are suspended in a place where the only thing to do is to get in touch with the teachings and with ourselves. That's all—very clearly to get in touch. Every day we chant the Three Refuges: "I take refuge in the Buddha. I take refuge in the Dharma. I take refuge in the Sangha." There is much talk these days of support systems. We have a wonderful support system. The Buddha, a human being who practiced faithfully and who came to understand the true nature of the universe and of himself, said to all of us, "You can do this, too." The Dharma is the teaching of our everyday life experience, right here. The Sangha is our companionship, our being present for each other. And with our own richness of experience, we come little by little to feel true peace of mind, true contentment of spirit. Each of us is the only one who can know if this is so.

---

*In *Namu Dai Bosa: A Transmission of Zen to America,* edited by Louis Nordstrom, Senzaki writes: "For seventeen years I simply walked many stages of American life, making myself a grass of the field, meditating alone in Golden Gate Park, or studying hard in the Public Library of San Francisco. Whenever I could save money, I would hire a hall and give a talk on Buddhism—this started in 1922. I called our meeting place at that time a 'floating Zendo.' "

†An adaptation from Senzaki's own account in *The Iron Flute* (Rutland, Vermont: Charles E. Tuttle Co., 1964), p. 58.

Thanks to this practice, I feel I do have some true peace of mind. After all, life and death, health and illness are one. The true face of this universe includes all things in it—good, bad, life, death, health, illness—all of it. There are many so-called healers in the world, but healers cannot bring us wholeness. Healers do not heal us. The healing is already there in the wholeness. And the real goal of healing is to help the person in need of healing to be aware of this. At the deepest level, the so-called sick person has no sickness. At this level, I am not sick.* With deep gratitude to this practice—because of Buddha, Dharma, Sangha; because of all of you; because of all of this that we are engaged in together; because of this indefinable, mysteriously unspeakable, marvelous whatever-it-is—I really do feel this no-sickness.

You cannot take my definition, my experience of it, as yours, of course. The only reason I tell you of my experience is in the hope that it may encourage you. It is your own life experience that confronts you all the time. Your heart doesn't beat because you think about it. Your breath is not breathing because you say, "breathe." A power beyond definition is making our hearts beat and making us breathe. This is the reality of our lives.

So we know why we are here. We are here to get rid of confusion. Each of us must do it. Buddha said, "You must be a lamp unto yourself." May our lamps shine out, unselfconsciously, so that we may continue this wonderful practice for all beings.

---

*Maurine's medical tests had indicated metastasized cancer. This talk was given January 23, 1989, one year before her death.

15

Peace of Mind

BODHIDHARMA WAS already an old man when he made the long three-year journey from India to China in 520 C.E., and the story of what happened when he paid his respects to the Emperor Wu is well known. The emperor thought of himself as a very good Buddhist. He had built monasteries, he had seen to it that sacred texts were transcribed, he had done many things that he considered exceptionally fine. But when he asked Bodhidharma about the merit due him for all of this, much to his shock and surprise, Bodhidharma said, "No merit. None."

If you do something for the sake of merit, there is no merit. The work you do inconspicuously that nobody ever knows you did is the work that is really the most meaningful. Work that is done not for the sake of an expected reward, but for the sake of the work itself, for the sake of the next person who comes along, is work that is worthy. When you go to the bathroom, you leave everything as clean, neat, and orderly as you found it. If you didn't find it that way, you make it that way for the next person. That is true compassion.

After his encounter with the emperor, Bodhidharma went off to a cave among some impressive cliffs. He sat down facing the wall, just as we do. There he sat, for nine years. One day during that time, along came Eka, who had heard about this strange blue-eyed monk from India. Although Eka had studied the Chinese classics, knew Chinese poetry, had memorized the sutras, and had attended lectures by the dozens—just as most of us have done—for all that learning, he still did not have any peace of mind. So he arrived at Bodhidharma's place, at Shorinji, and asked to be taught.

What did Bodhidharma say? "No, I won't teach you. The subtle and supreme teaching of the Buddhas can be understood only through doing what is hard to do and bearing what is hard to bear. How can a person of little virtue and much self-conceit dream of achieving this? Go away!"

What would you do if somebody said that to you? This was a test, of course. To this day, this test is used to some degree. *Niwazume,* the three days of sitting outside the monastery gate before being accepted, is a way of finding out what your intention is. Why are you sitting here? Why are you sitting in this sesshin from dawn until nine o'clock in the evening?

Eka's intention was quite strong. He stood in the snow and was rejected time after time, and finally it is said that he cut off his arm. This is only a symbol, of course. It meant that he was ready to give up his life. "My mind has no peace. Please help me," he begged Bodhidharma.

Bodhidharma said, "Bring your mind here and I will pacify it for you." Eka said, "I have searched for my mind, and I cannot take hold of it." Bodhidharma said, "Now your mind is pacified."

There is no mind to find, no fixed condition. We cannot put the mind in a little cubbyhole and say, "There, now I have peace of mind." We have all felt this yearning for inner calm. But nobody can help us. We must do it ourselves. We have to face our own inner demons; nobody can do that for us. We have to deal with our grabby ego, continually trying to fix everything in some permanent condition, which prevents us from having peace of mind. We are convinced that our way is the right way, and therefore that nobody else's way is the right way, and so we become anxious, ill at ease, angry, "raising waves where there is no wind," as Mumon says in his commentary on this story from the *Gateless Gate.*

Sitting on the cushion, we are making arguments in our minds. What am I doing here? Am I doing this the right way or am I wrong? Does she like what I did? Does he approve? We are raising waves, disturbing our minds instead of being so completely involved in what we are doing that we cannot have any second thoughts about it. Instead of just washing the floor or dusting the cushions, while we're working we're thinking. "Oh, I have to go to work tomorrow. I wonder what my boss will say," and on and on. We use up so much life energy in this anxiety-producing mental activity, raising waves where there's no wind.

Dogen gave some wonderful advice about thoughts arising in zazen: "When a thought arises be awake to it. When you are awake to it, it will disappear. After a long time the associations are destroyed, and spontaneously, there is a coming to One. This is the secret of zazen." Zazen is not about trying to stop our thoughts, but about being clearly awake to them. For example, we hear various sounds, and our minds shift toward them. Without trying to suppress this shifting of the mind, we should inquire, What is this sound? Where did it come from? What is this idea? Who is thinking about it? In this way, we can become aware of the disturbances of the mind. By doing this over and over, thoughts and fantasies vanish. After a time, continuing this kind of meditation not just for one or two days but for years and years and years, the associations are destroyed. The subject and the object, which are joined by association, just disappear. The subject is the mind; the object is its counterpart, the Buddha-field in which sound is heard. Likewise with what is seen: the seer is the subject; the seen is the object. As we continue this kind of awareness practice, the experience and the experiencer disappear. And the disappearance of these two is their spontaneous coming together, through which we experience the One. In deep samadhi, our zazen is nothing but this oneness: gateless gateness. It is nothing but inner and outer, in-breath and out-breath, just this.

Life is suffering, the Buddha taught, because we want some permanency, some guarantee. If we let go of this desire and just follow a path of doing finite things in an infinite way, then ordinary becomes extraordinary; secular is sacred. Preparing the food, washing the dishes; everything is a sacred act.

This path must be followed without any shortcuts. Unlike instant coffee, enlightenment isn't bought in a jar. We must walk on our own two feet, alone. And when we come to the zendo to sit together for an evening or for sesshin, we are loving, supportive companions for each other. This gives us more courage to go on alone. It is our own body, our own breath through which we experience each moment fully. The effect that we have on one another is very strong; we feel our interrelatedness very clearly. So be mindful. What is our thought? What is our intention?

Someone told me she has been finding it very difficult to follow the Ten Precepts. Of course it is difficult to follow this path unswervingly. But the Three Fundamental Precepts offer very simple, very clear directions: Refrain from bad acts. Do good acts as much as possible. Keep your mind pure and warm. When our minds are Mu-shin—emptied out, cleared up—then we cannot hurt anyone. We cannot really act in an inappropriate way, because we feel our interrelatedness.

Why are we here? Are we here for some self-improvement? Zen is not psychotherapy. Are we here, warming and purifying our minds, for the sake of all sentient beings? D. T. Suzuki once said, "Buddhists have almost nothing to do with Buddha, but very much to do with their fellow beings." And the great Christian mystic Meister Eckhart, a true Zen man, said, "If a person were in such a rapturous state as St. Paul once entered, and he knew of a sick man who needed a cup of soup, it would be better to withdraw from the rapture for love's sake to serve him who is in need." This is true Zen spirit, true bodhisattva spirit. We are not here to grab something, to get something. Zen insight is not *our* awareness, but the Buddha-mind's awareness in us.

Someone told me he was very embarrassed when complimented about his artwork; he became quite self-conscious, and didn't know what to say. I told him, "When somebody says to me, 'You play the piano beautifully,' I say, 'Yes, I do. Thank you. I really do play beautifully, but *I* don't play. Something plays me.' " The more we come to the condition of emptied-out, cleared-up, warmed-up mind, the more easily we can let go of the self-consciousness that makes us denigrate ourselves, or worry about seeming conceited. We can be glad we can make something beautiful or play beautifully; we can be glad to share it with others, and glad they like it. It is not conceited to say, "Yes, I play the piano beautifully." If I did not, after all the training, all the work, all the effort, it would be sad. And so it is with you. Each of you is the artist of your own life. Play your life beautifully. Hold your head up and be glad that you can offer whatever it is you have to offer, freely.

A little bell hanging in the emptiness sings. Each one of us is hanging in the emptiness, singing. Sometimes lover, sometimes wife, sometimes husband, sometimes artist, sometimes friend; always with open, compassionate wisdom minds.

16

No Big Deal

OUR ZEN LIFE is ordinary life. When we start adding things to it, as Nyogen Senzaki said, it's like "painting legs on a snake." Just to be ordinary is the most difficult thing. To be plain, to be simple, not to make a fuss about anything, this is our Zen life.

Joshu, one of the greatest teachers, always used whatever was at hand. His teachings were along the lines of, "Have you eaten your porridge? Have you washed your bowls?" Of course, when such ordinary acts are done thoroughly, completely, cheerfully, then they become extraordinary. Every single bite of porridge is tasted, fully. But it is not done with the feeling of doing something special. There is no self-congratulatory inner voice saying, "Oh, look! I'm such a wonderful Zen student, sitting long hours, doing everything so mindfully." We just do it, with no thought about it, whatever it is. To draw attention to what we are doing would be sickening, and would have nothing to do with Zen.

We just wash our bowls, washing away any excessive use of Zen terminology, any allusions to enlightenment. For our practice to become more ordinary, more real, we use words that everybody can understand. We refer to what is right here, right now. We sit, we walk, we cook, we eat, we clean, we have nose-bleeds, and it's just here, right in front of us. No big deal.

Practicing together is a wonderful, extraordinary experience, yet we are so much in it that we can't even talk about it. There is nothing to say. Every single act, everything we do is the expression of our true nature. We may not know it, we may not be aware of it, we may not even think we have any insight, but everything we do is an expression of who we are: standing up, sitting down, eating, drinking, laughing, crying, washing our bowls. Especially if we do it unself-consciously.

And we have never done any of it before. This is the first sitting, the first kinhin we have ever experienced. We are fresh, completely fresh, taking nothing for granted, with no ideas about what Zen is. Everything is seen as if for the very first time. Even though the sesshin schedule may be very familiar to some of us, we are going through it with keen attention, really being present with each moment, really eating our porridge, really washing our bowls. And when it's done, it's done. There's nothing to hold on to. Nothing.

Nor do we hold anything back. We don't think, "Next time things will be easier, I'll work harder, I'll be able to concentrate better, I'll do better." Right now is all we have. That's it. So let's be here. Let's burn up our resources unstintingly. When we think we have something, we just forget about it. We start all over again, going deeper and deeper, never thinking we have completely understood. Sometimes people ask me, "When did you finish your Zen training?" I have never finished. There's no end to it. When we think we have attained something, we're in trouble. We need to wash away everything and become a beginner over and over and over again.

A young woman called me this week from California to tell me she had cancer. Very worried, very upset, she said, "I am preparing to die." I said, "How about preparing to live? They go together." And then I asked her, "Do you know any people who need help?" She said, "Lots." I told her, "Well, you'd better get busy. Don't worry about your lump. Find somebody else to help." Later, it turned out that what this young woman thought was cancer was just a benign tumor.

Once there was a monk who spent three years at the famous master Hogen's place without going to see him. Finally Hogen asked him why he never came to him to inquire about Buddhism. The monk said, "Before this I was with Master Seiho, and I heard the doctrine and attained peace and bliss."

Hogen asked him what words had brought him this peace, and the monk said he had asked Seiho, "How is it, the self of this disciple?" Seiho had responded, "The lamp boy is looking for the light."

Hogen said, "Well, that's a very nice phrase, but you probably have not understood it." So the monk, a little bit angered that his wonderful realization was being questioned, told Hogen, "Well, this is how I understand it. The lamp boy is in charge of the lights. Taking the light to go to look for the light is like my taking the self to look for the self." Hogen said, "I knew it. You have not understood at all. If that were Buddhism, it would never have lasted until now."

The monk was very upset. He got up at once and started to leave, thinking to himself, "What am I doing studying under such a fool? He doesn't even see how wonderful my understanding is!" After going a little way, it occurred to him that this Hogen was supposed to be a man of great spiritual attainment, one of the wisest teachers around. So maybe there was something to what he said. So he went back, and this time, he said, "I have been wrong. I bow and ask pardon. In reverence and repentance I ask, 'How is it, the self of this disciple?'"

Hogen replied, "The lamp boy is looking for the light." And with this, suddenly, the monk had true enlightenment.

What happened? The first time the monk was dwelling in the realm of the intellect, of concepts, of somebody else's words, some prepared answer. "Taking the self to look for the self" was his imitative way of saying, "The self is the Buddha," and was no more than painting a picture. And when Hogen rejected his answer, the monk's angry reaction was a confirmation that he really hadn't understood. Yet he went back and he asked Hogen's pardon. This is the point, the essential matter: that he let go of his egocentric self, to allow himself to become one with his teacher. When he asked Hogen's pardon, those words were his own.

So it is with us. Some of you come and give me very fine phrases. But where do they come from? Are they your own? Are they from your own experience? If they are, they come forth in a very different way from phrases taken from a book or from someone else's words. What is your living experience of this? How do you express it? Yesterday I asked somebody to sing me a song. Quick! Right on the spot. And the person did. No self-consciousness, no "Oh, I'm nervous, I can't perform, I'm not good enough, I don't know it yet." It happened to be a Bach aria. It was a fresh, clear expression of this Mu practice. It was spontaneous and beautiful.

When we let go of all our intellectual stuff, all our indirect and static knowledge, we allow ourselves to get in touch with the dynamic and direct intuitive understanding that we all have. And out of this comes real freedom, freedom to express whatever is in the moment. Like the burglar who locked his son in a chest as a way of teaching him his trade, a good Zen teacher puts the student in a box from which there seems to be no way out. The student must find the answer in his or her own way.

The more we practice, the more we come to know our own minds, and we come to realize the absolute hopelessness of the mind restrained by the ego. All our accumulated knowledge is inadequate. Our teacher tells us over and over again, "Be simple, be plain, be ordinary, be open, have no fixed ideas," and still, we hang on to the idea that we can achieve something. Finally, we give it up. A young man told me he was walking, step after step after step, and how wonderful it was. Finally, he had given up the idea that he had to do something. When we completely surrender into this, then everything goes quite smoothly. When we give up the egoistic effort, when we stop saying, "I have certain standards" or "I demand such and such from myself," then we can do the very best we can. We walk with full concentration in the moment, and let everything else take care of itself.

Something else that must be given up is the idea of labeling. This universe, and everything in it including ourselves, is in a flowing situation. There are no fixed identities. The true Buddhist doesn't say, "I am a Buddhist," or "I am a Zen Buddhist," or "I am a Tibetan Buddhist." We are just human beings. When the Buddha was asked to give a definition of reality, he didn't put any label on it. He referred to "ongoing," to "not becoming," "not made," "not compounded." He directed us to look into matters of our own experience, to examine the nature of suffering. Where does our suffering come from? "My way." "My opinion." "This is the way things should be." "I have to do it this way." When we let go of this egoistic way of life, we discover what Obaku said: "Mind, universal mind, or reality, is no other than the Buddha, and Buddha is no other than sentient beings. When mind assumes the form of sentient beings it has suffered no decrease, and when it has become a Buddha it has added nothing to itself."

So clear away these deep-seated notions that a real, substantiated, and abiding ego exists. Thank goodness it does not. It did not, and it will not. What a relief! As we go along in this practice, we begin to see things differently. But don't expect anything. Don't think, "My life will change dramatically." To say, "My life . . ." is to go back to that egoistic process. Just do what needs to be done, and let the results take care of themselves. Be patient. Everything will change.

17

Daily Life Practice
Is the Way

OFTEN, WHEN A student comes to see me, I ask, "How is your everyday-life koan going?" Our strong, formal Zen training helps us live our ordinary lives supremely well, to the best of our ability—not making inordinate demands of ourselves, but accepting what we can do, step by step; not being discouraged because things do not go as perfectly as we think they should go, but being patient and mindful, and observing how this condition changes, moment after moment, sitting after sitting. One minute we may be very sad, depressed about something that we feel we have not done very well. In the next moment, we realize that after all we must drop it and move on. That moment presents something else, and then something else again. Being constantly aware of impermanence—how helpful that is in our lives!

A monk named Ro Joza was once lifting a kettle for the tea ceremony when he accidentally overturned it. "What is under the kettle?" asked the government official for whom Ro was making tea. What makes us have accidents? What has caused the overturning of the kettle? Do we allow an accident to knock us off base, or do we just keep steadily moving on?

In each koan, some words are very important and some are not so important. In this one, watch out for what is under the kettle. Watch out for what is under your feet! Maintain your firm awareness of mind and body, wherever you are.

Sosan, the Third Patriarch, says in his poem "On Believing in Mind,"

> One in All
> All in One—
> If only this is realized,
> No more worry about your not being perfect!

No more worry about tipping over the pot during the tea ceremony, or keeping things in some pristine condition. "If only this is realized," we are able to regain our balance moment after moment. We are not knocked off base by the little mishaps that come up in our life. We are not wallowing in them, not indulging in self-pity.

Daily-life practice is the Way. This is the hardest practice. But if we think of the tea ceremony, it may help. What is under that kettle that's warming the water in your life? What is the firm foundation that you are making now, sitting in this strong zazen posture, following your breath, letting all the extraneous stuff fall off? This is what we are doing: making a wonderful, firm base for the kettle. And if the kettle gets spilled, if some accident occurs, we maintain our firm footing, our Mu-shin.

In the story about the overturning of the teakettle, Ro Joza's teacher, Myosho, says, "Still you wander about the countryside, working with a stump." He means, Why are you not getting down to essential matters? Why are you not really devoting yourself to this great matter? Ro answers, "What about you?"

Don't ask someone else. Please work on your own original answer in life. Take care of your own life; drive your own life. Get on with your own affairs. Once when I went to see Soen

Roshi he asked, "How did you get here?" "I drove my car," I replied. And he asked me, "How are you driving your life?"

You may wonder, "What about this matter of pain, desire, all of that?" In the *Heart Sutra,* we read that the Prajna Paramita Dharani "completely clears all suffering." But to have no pain and no desire is not to become dead. In fact, it means to have no connection with selfishness. This is where our pain comes from. Often we feel pain for others' suffering. But the pain of dissatisfaction and depression is connected with selfish ideas. Of course sometimes we have to be selfish to some extent, as in protecting our space, our health, our time. But when this small self just stays small, and does not expand to more than itself, then indeed there is pain. When this small self finds itself enveloped in that wider and deeper being, then it is not merely a relative self, and we can accept the pains of everyday life with more courage, more endurance. *This* is what Zen gives us.

There are two Buddhist terms, known as *ri* and *ji* in Japanese. *Ri* means universal truth. *Ji* means a particular event or phenomenon. Another way of saying it is formlessness and form. Ji also means a technique that can be seen and taught. But what is formless cannot be seen or taught, or even chosen. The ji of zazen, the instruction in how to practice, is very simple, very plain, very straightforward. But there is a deeper meaning of this instruction with respect to posture and breathing. Our attitude toward life is expressed in our posture. Each one of us knows by the condition of our own breath what is going on in our minds—our composure or lack of composure. Ri shows itself in every situation. It is expressed not only in wonderful Zen calligraphy, but in our lives, in the art of living. I cannot do calligraphy, but I have practiced the piano over and over and over; I have done really deep practice, and have always considered it my spiritual practice from the earliest days of my life. So instead of doing calligraphy for you, I may say, "Would you like to hear a Bach 'Prelude and Fugue'?" That is my Zen expression.

The point of using one special Way again and again is that our expression becomes clearer and clearer through the discipline, just as with zazen, sitting after sitting, everything becomes clearer. When we are in the condition of Mu-shin, even to some small degree, then nature and spirit, human and superhuman become one; then great works of art are created. Looking at a calligraphy by Soen Roshi, we feel how Mu wrote Mu. There has been no egocentric attempt at effect, no interference, but simply a spontaneous and wonderfully vivid expression that comes straight out at us. There is no fixing it up, no removing the smudges, no brushing it over—it's just as it is.

The ego is the natural enemy of all great human activity. When it is out of the way, we are in a heavenly condition. In this state of selflessness, our energy makes the heavens dance: not choosing to do, but being done. In the T'ang period, the golden age of Zen in China, there were no koans, there were just living situations. Any time, any place was the place of practice. Everything at hand, every event was an occasion for the forceful and free functioning of Zen. So it is in our lives. Any time, any place is our place of practice. It's wonderful to have a zendo to come to, but in fact we carry our zendo within us, everywhere we go.

18

Asking Why

W E ARE ALWAYS asking questions. What is the noise outside? What are they doing in the kitchen? Why is she
late? What happened today? And children ask questions from
their very first word. Why? Why do you do that? Why is this
so? Why is the sun up there? What makes it shine? What is the
snow? Another question, and another, and coming from all the
questions, more questions. An answer provokes another question. Each of us has questions: Why am I here? What am I
going to do about this aspect of my life? How do I clear
this up?

Many of our questions come from dividing subject and object. Our deep-rooted and ingrained habit is to make pictures,
graven images, so as to render perceptible, and set up as permanent, what is imperceptible and ineffable: sunyata, or emptiness.
Emptiness is a name for something that can not be designated,
because it does not exist relative to other things. Emptiness
means that which has no permanent form and can thus manifest
in any form. Or it could also be said that things are emptiness
having become form. That itself is the gist of the *Heart Sutra:*
"Form is emptiness; emptiness is form."

The Bodhisattva Avalokitesvara, who appears in the *Heart Sutra,* is the bodhisattva of compassion and wisdom, and is often depicted as having one thousand hands and one thousand eyes: one thousand eyes to see the thousands of needs, and one thousand hands to help. Some depictions have eleven faces as well, to symbolize seeing in all directions simultaneously. There is a story about this:

One day, Mayoku asked Rinzai, "Avalokitesvara has one thousand hands, and each has an eye. Which is the real eye?" Rinzai repeated the question, saying, "Now tell me! Quick!" Mayoku pulled Rinzai from his seat and sat in his place. Rinzai stood up and asked, "Why?", and then shouted "Kwatz!" and pulled Mayoku from his seat.

Rinzai's response was immediate and spontaneous. Why? Why are you asking which is the true eye? Why? Why? Why are we here? "Why" is my favorite question.

All the different roles that each one of us represents—man, woman, friend, artist, mother, lover, child, whatever—every single one is this true eye, without exception. We are expressing this true eye, working with whatever we are doing at this moment with this "Why?", this shout. This moment-to-moment experience of being here is what is so vital to all of us. To answer this "Why?" in our own way, with our own experience, without any speculation, is what we are here to do.

There was a nun in the Rinzai School who was given *inka*—that means she was given transmission from her teacher and allowed to teach—and some of the monks were a little hesitant about this. Was it all right for that lady to give a discourse on the *Rinzai Roku?* Is it all right for this piano player from Saskatchewan, Canada, to be up here giving a talk on the *Rinzai Roku?*

Well, that nun, Shido, who was the founder of Tokei-ji, was confronted by the head monk, who did not at all approve of her having been given inka. He decided to question her. Aha, I will trap her and show how stupid this lady is, he thought; I will show that she is not ready to be a *Rinzai Roku* teacher. So he said to her, "In our line, one who receives inka gives a discourse on the *Rinzai Roku*. Can this nun really brandish the staff of the Dharma in the Dharma seat?"

Shido faced him. She drew out her ten-inch knife, which was carried by all women of her warrior class, and she held it up. She said, "Certainly a Zen teacher of the line of the patriarchs should go up on the high seat and speak on this book. But I am a woman of the warrior line, and I should declare our teaching face-to-face with the drawn sword. What book should I need?"

The head monk then said, "Before father and mother are born, with what then will you declare our teaching?" The nun closed her eyes and sat perfectly still.

Each one of us, in our dynamic, wonderful presence, is the living *Rinzai Roku*. My living *Rinzai Roku* is to be here with you, heart to heart. This is what Rinzai asks us to do—not to hang on to words and phrases, but to reveal our own living, dynamic spirit. This is what we are here for.

What is this spirit? What is this American Zen that we are practicing? The founders of the Cambridge Buddhist Association were D. T. Suzuki, Shinichi Hisamatsu, Elsie and John Mitchell, and some other wonderful people. One of the things Dr. Hisamatsu said when it was founded was, "I stress the flexibility of Zen. One must know something of its history to understand it, but one must also be aware of its flexibility, of the way it adapts to various circumstances. It is not rigid, and it must be able to change its form from what it was a century ago."

How will Zen differ from what it was? What is happening to Zen in America? Some of what is going on is difficult, and because of that, it is making us grow up in our Zen practice; making us less dependent; making us see things much more clearly.

Before Zen came to America, there was already a great deal of feeling in Japan that it needed to be less encrusted by temple stuff, although there is nothing intrinsically wrong with a temple. But the feeling was that Zen should extend itself to lay-people, and not just to men but to women too. One of the Zen masters in Japan who believed this strongly was Kosen Imakita, who was born in 1816. He was extremely interested in Western culture, and insisted that his monks go to the university and learn about other parts of the world, study other languages and philosophies; in fact, open their minds. It was he who was the teacher of Soyen Shaku, who was the first Zen master to come to America in 1893, when he gave a talk at the World Parliament of Religions in Chicago. Soyen Shaku came understanding our language, understanding a great deal about Western thought. He was very much appreciated by those who heard him speak, and was asked to come back. So in 1905 he returned and stayed for awhile in San Francisco, which became the seat of Zen practice in America. He was welcomed into the home of Mrs. Alexander Russell. She was the first person in America to study Zen.

Another great Zen lady in our American tradition is Elsie Mitchell. When I first came to the Cambridge Buddhist Association, it was she who insisted on giving me everything to do that she possibly could. It was a great way of taking me out of my loneliness, my malaise at having to leave New York City, where I had such a wonderful Zen practice. I had felt a deep dissatisfaction at having to leave. Soen Roshi had said to me, "Do not be so sad; find Elsie Mitchell and you will be all right." Indeed, he was right.

Recently, I was asked by a group of women in California to lead a sesshin just for women. I said, "I am absolutely at your disposal. I am very fond of men and would love to have them with us. But if you feel that there will be some special quality, something we can experience together as women, then let us do it, and find out what happens." So we did. It was held at a retreat house in Marin County, a quiet, beautifully cared for place with white deer wandering around on the front lawn, with hummingbirds in every little flower. It was an incredible paradise. But the meditation room of this center was not for us Zen students. It was very heavily carpeted, and each little tuft of carpet was full of rose incense, and the windows would not open wide enough.

So we moved all the furniture out of the living room, which was right next door to the kitchen, and right next door to the dining room. What about the noise of food preparation and setting the table and so on? Everything flowed into everything else, in a wonderful way. People did most of their preparation at times when we were not sitting, but some work had to be done during zazen, and it was, quietly. We went from the zendo to the dining room, which was right there, and to the kitchen, which was right there, and back into the zendo, and it was all wonderfully loving. We had a great time together. The atmosphere became stronger and warmer; everyone felt less and less judgmental.

Many of these women had been intimidated by the atmosphere of sesshin in the past, and also felt somewhat fearful because of certain things that had happened regarding relationships with teachers. But sitting here together, we all felt closer, freer. We listened to Rinzai, we listened to Nansen and to Joshu as if they were there—as they were.

As they are: the spirit is here, not in ancient China. It is present in our time and our place, right here. We are listening to Nansen telling Joshu that this calm and ordinary mind, this nondiscriminating mind, is the Way; and hearing Rinzai encourage us to seek Buddha within ourselves. It is not something we seek outside, not something given to us by someone. Rinzai is telling us to free ourselves from him, from attachment to him or to any teacher. It is so easy for us to become attached to someone or something we revere. We put someone up on a pedestal. Soen Roshi was absolutely adamant about this. He always said, "Do not put me in that place. I am just an ordinary monk. I have to practice harder than you, so please don't put me in that place. Have no attachment to me. Look at the universe, look at the stars, look at the moon, look at all of this in front of you; don't look to me."

As long as we look outside, it's no good, no matter how lofty the teacher is. In so far as that presence is outside us, it's not our own treasure. We come together to realize Rinzai in *us,* and to hear his wonderful shout as our shout of joy in celebrating life together. This "kwatz!" is to be danced to. And his "Why?" is always wondering in us, just like Soen Roshi's phrase, "Endless dimension universal life," no beginning and no end, just wondering, "Why?". When one of my children started mathematics in grade school, she had a remarkable teacher who wrote on her report card, "At the beginning of the term, Barbara caught the spirit of mathematics and wondered on."

Dogen Zenji said, "If you cannot find a true teacher, it is better not to practice." Who, or what, is the true teacher? Our practice, whatever it is, is our teacher. This does not necessarily mean Zen practice; each of us here has our own practice. Our life is our practice, our koan. Each one of us learns from our own life, if we listen deeply, if we are involved to the very bottom of it. This is our true teacher, our most venerable teacher.

And what is our attitude toward this teacher? Are we sitting with dependency, with thoughts of gaining something, with grabby feelings? Or is our practice openhearted, no-knowing, giving oneself up, moment-after-moment open, so that whatever comes, whether good, bad, beautiful, or ugly, we don't make a move to avoid it?

At that women's sesshin in California, afterward we sat around in a circle and had a very intimate time. People were ready to share their experiences with one another, in a feeling of freedom and compassion for one another, of deep compassion. Some women had wept during that sesshin; some had faced enormous crises. Each one of us was there, really there, with them. What came out of that was a feeling of real strength. Our compassion and wisdom were gentle and strong; we were women warriors, cutting off all our delusions about what we could or could not be. There we were.

19

Who Is the Real You?

O UR ESSENTIAL NATURE is no different from that of the buddhas; the substance of the universe is coextensive with our own Buddha-nature. When our minds are clouded with delusion, however, we don't see this. We see nothing but a world of individual entities. We are unaware that we are never separate from our essential Buddha-nature, whether we realize it or not.

When we hear that we are endowed with Buddha-nature from the very beginning, we want to know where it is. We begin our search for our true nature. We begin by reading books, listening to talks; and gradually, a firm belief in the reality of Buddha-nature comes about. Then we are driven to discover it with all the force of our being. And when we do, what is it that we have discovered? Only that we have never been without it.

Sitting down and concentrating one's mind on a single matter, nothing is left unrealized. This does not mean that we control our minds. Our minds naturally settle down through our practice of mindfulness. Instead of drifting around, we truly turn our attention inward. Instead of the "monkey-mind" condition—scrambling about from thought to thought—we just sit.

We concentrate on one thing: following the breath, or counting the breaths, or just letting Mu do Mu.

Our minds naturally settle down if we let them. If we can get rid of our egocentric preoccupation that *we* have to *do* something, then Mu does Mu. The body takes up its natural posture, the breath flows all by itself, and all inner and outer disturbances resolve themselves. When we try to resolve them, they only become stickier. There's nothing to do but to be ordinary, plain, and take one thing at a time.

Rinzai says, "The mind is without form; it pervades the ten directions, and is functioning right before your eyes." These are not just words for us to memorize or quote; this is a vivid expression of the mind revealing itself. Can you see it? Are you experiencing it? Are you it? Without form, it is pervading the ten directions, manifesting itself right here before us. It is no different from what runs around seeking it. It shows itself right here, whether we can see it or not. It is not a matter of believing or not believing, knowing or not knowing, seeing or not seeing. It is beyond that.

The way of being truly human is beyond all shapes. It has no form. When we use words like "Buddha" or "Tathagata" there is some danger that we think of this as something apart from us. Searching for the mystery outside oneself leads us astray. The mystery is right here.

Are you completely here, or is part of you somewhere else? Are you all of a piece or are you split? Each of you has different roles in this life, each of you wears many different hats, but are you fundamentally aware of your own true person? Who is the real you? There is no unchanging ego, there is no entity called a soul. Everything is constantly changing in the stream of cause and effect. What has appeared vividly one moment is gone the next. Moment after moment, it streams along. Beyond this coming and going, this appearing and disappearing, there is nothing else. Phenomena are coming and going, and when you ask what is real, you have already missed it. It's gone. What is real is only realized in deep zazen, deep samadhi. We pass from one conditioned state of mind to another. Dark, cloudy moments come, tears come, and then the sun comes out, and we smile; the mind is clear and then again it's troubled, it's in pain. All is just passing by. The mind is like the sky. A bird flies in, flies out. A cloud floats in, floats out. An airplane comes in, goes out. We are just here, quietly and earnestly doing zazen. With this understanding, no matter what kind of situation we get into, we find our base is strong. When things become clear, who is the real you?

People have said to me, "It's all very well to come to the zendo and sit in peace and quiet, but what do we do when we go home?" That's the big test, the big koan, for all of us. How do we deal with this everyday life? We think, "I have so many passions, so many things that upset me, so much going on in my life; how do I find peace of mind?" Dogen said that when the clay is plentiful, the buddha is big. He meant by clay, raw passion—lots of it. Where does the lotus grow? In the mud. If someone tells me, "I never get angry, I don't have any jealousy in my nature," I think, "Oh, really?" We are constantly dealing with such emotions, and they fertilize our practice. So please do not feel that you have to be in some absolutely tranquil, serene, permanently detached condition. This is not possible. It is not human. But because of this practice, when some deep emotion like anger takes hold, when your whole body is blazing with it, then in the very midst of it you taste Mu; you realize the true peace of mind that has been there all along. You have never been without it.

20

The Naked Truth

Somebody asked me about enlightenment. We don't talk about enlightenment; we are here to experience it, to have deeper and deeper insight into this moment. Our practice, our study, is the realization of the living Buddha-dharma at this moment. It is Buddha-dharma as it presents itself in every aspect of our lives; as it expresses itself right now in all its vitality.

We who study Buddha-dharma, who seek true insight, must understand that the true way of seeking is not to seek at all. To seek true insight in this way is to become what Rinzai called the "true person without rank"—to live directly, here and now, right now. This "true person" is vividly present.

One day, Rinzai took his seat in the Dharma hall and said, "On this lump of red flesh there is a true person without rank, who is always going in and out of the face of each one of you." A monk asked, "What about the true person without rank?" He wanted an explanation. Rinzai got down, grabbed the monk, and said, "Speak, speak!" The monk couldn't say anything. Rinzai said, "What kind of shit-wiping stick is he?" and left the room. It was not an explanation, but a direct demonstration of "true person" that Rinzai gave that monk.

When you come to see me in the dokusan room, how do you present this true person? Not by looking outside yourself, not by giving me some long discourse. This true person is right here. The monk was oblivious, and tried to get Rinzai to talk about it. But this was not Rinzai's way, and this is not Zen. Zen is a heart-to-heart, mind-to-mind, dynamic transmission. Talking about it is just doctrinal instruction. There's no Zen in that.

Rinzai, grabbing the monk, said, "Speak, speak! Who is this true person? Show me!" Again, Rinzai's person was functioning freely, directly contacting this questioning monk. But the monk couldn't respond vividly and spontaneously to this wonderful moment. How many moments do we lose because we are so self-conscious? If he could have forgotten himself and opened up to the moment, he might have really experienced this true person without rank and come to a great realization. But being dependent upon some word of explanation, he didn't know what to do or say. Surprised, he couldn't act. We, too, sometimes feel we must have some set of instructions, or we don't know what to do or say. This is certainly not the Zen way, certainly not Rinzai's way. This way is to be independent. When you walk, walk. When you sit, sit. When you shit, shit!

"Your true person without rank, what kind of shit-wiping stick is he?" Rinzai said to this monk, who was completely entangled, completely caught up in some idea of a true person outside himself. With these abrupt words, Rinzai snatched away this idea. Swinging his sleeves, he returned to his room. Again, Rinzai's true person showed himself to the monk with great vitality. He presented with such clarity the essence, the marrow, the ultimate ground of all Buddhist teaching, right there. And the monk was still asleep. How about you?

When we ask a conceptual question the way that monk did, we are distancing ourselves from the dynamic functioning of the true presence of things just as they are. This one true person without rank functions freely, going and returning without being caught anywhere. Anything that gets caught cannot be this true person. Rinzai is not separated from us. As a historical figure, of course, he lived more than one thousand years ago. But the one true person without rank is each of us. So that we can know this, not through words, but really know it, we must experience this one true person, and that is why we are practicing zazen. All the simple, ordinary, everyday things we do— walking, cleaning, sitting—are ways to deeply penetrate this.

We are not doing this practice to gain some superficial composure; we are not here to feel a little bit better physically. These things may happen, but they are by-products. Gaining true insight is what we are here for. And then we can live our lives unaffected by living and dying. Living and dying includes everything. Not just our own life and death—everything, everything is living and dying, moment after moment.

When we gain true insight into this, then we can freely come, freely go, without getting entangled, without being deluded by others; then we can endlessly transform ourselves, without becoming caught up in the ongoing transformation. Letting it come, letting it go. In the midst of impermanence, we are constantly changing without getting enmeshed in any of it. This is what we are here to experience. We are not here to talk about it, but to experience it. This is absolute freedom, not relative freedom—it's not just being free from a few icky, sticky things.

Ultimate freedom is what we are here for. Ultimate, absolute freedom is what comes with true insight. And again, we do not come by this true insight by trying to become free. The very trying is an impediment. In our trying, we become grabby; we want something; we want to become enlightened. In seeking some supreme state of mind, some supernormal powers, we get caught in the leaves and branches, instead of going directly to the root.

In truth, there is nothing to do. But we are *doing* nothing, *doing, doing, doing,* vividly. We are not sitting on the cushion daydreaming; we are not just passively letting things happen.

We are dynamically present to them. Then everything becomes quite extraordinary. Somebody told me he'd like a few more sparkling events in his zazen. But if we are really present in our zazen, the whole thing is a sparkling event! Shining!

What do you think about enlightenment? Don't. Don't think about it even for one second. And don't look to someone else to do it for you. No teacher can give you true insight. True insight simply is. Each one of us must open up to this; each one of us must awaken to it. There is no other way to save anyone. A teacher can inspire us; reading his or her words may spark our energy, give us more stability, more endurance; but true insight is up to us.

We can't depend on Rinzai, or regard him as some kind of authority; he would hate that, and would hit us, hard. The authority is here, in us. He said, "Solitarily emancipated, and nondependent, go on your way." We are followers of the Way who are not dependent on the buddhas or ancestral teachers. Nor are we dependent upon the precepts. Taking the precepts is a wonderful commitment to our practice. But we do not awaken to this true person without rank by taking the precepts! All the many precepts return to the one precept at the source: the single-mind precept of Zen. Taking the precepts can inspire us to understand more, to experience more, to penetrate into this single-mind precept, which contains them all. There is no need to think, Am I doing well? Is this right or wrong? Freely flowing, we are each the true person without rank, with nothing to do in the midst of doing everything.

I always ask students who wish to take the precepts or become ordained, and I always ask myself when I am conducting such ceremonies, "Are you sure you are being completely honest with yourself? Why are you doing this? What is your real commitment to this?" This is not some mantle of authority that we put upon people. It is a deep responsibility to oneself and others. And since in truth there are no others—we are one with one another—there is no need even to say that.

True insight is pointing directly, heart to heart, mind to mind. We must not allow ourselves to be deluded by others, to be confused by others' actions or words. We must not place too much importance on words. Even the word "Dharma" can become an entanglement if we think of it as something outside ourselves. The Dharma is not outside ourselves; the Buddha is not outside ourselves. With true insight, we know who we are. To arrive at true insight, we simply don't wobble. We have faith in ourselves, realizing that each of us is the awakened one, right now.

Without faith in ourselves, we are tossed about here and there, willy-nilly. But this can turn around. We can feel the freedom in each moment, really feel that in the midst of pain, in the midst of sadness, in the midst of everything that life buffets us with, still, every day is a good day. It's O.K., just as it is, if we do not lack faith in ourselves, if instead of just tumbling along we open up to true insight.

How do we attain this insight? I don't continually come around with the stick and hit you; I don't say, "Kensho, kensho, kensho." I have experienced that approach myself, and I have found it singularly unhelpful. But you know what you are here for. Attain true insight, and you may make free use of every day. You will use things rather than be used by them. You will become the master. You will experience freedom in the midst of all the situations of your life, whatever they are; you will be truly composed. True composure is not just saying to yourself, "Be calm, quiet down now, everything is going to be O.K., just take a deep breath." It is not that. With true insight, there is no conscious trying to become composed. It's no use to try to do that. True composure is zazen condition taken into every circumstance of life. When the ceaselessly seeking mind is given up altogether, there is nothing to do. All we need to do is just be ordinary. Nansen said, "Ordinary mind is the Way." This ordinary mind does not go beyond distinctions of past and present, east and west, calm and constant. This mind is everywhere, in every time and place. It is never lacking for even a single instant. It pervades all things. So we sit, our 84,000 pores breathing in, breathing out, inhaling and exhaling, letting in the whole universe, going out to the whole universe. There is nothing to do. In this condition of mind, we can confront our life and death clearly, calmly.

Zen is not a puzzle. It is not something to be solved by our wits. It is a spiritual food for those who want to learn what life is, and what their mission in this world is. Mere scholarly pursuits will never lead to realization. Zen is not a philosophy, not a religion; it is the essence of life itself. The naked truth of the universe is none other than the experience of this essence. A person who has felt some deep inner uneasiness can come to Zen and find clear understanding, real joy. But Zen does not seek adherents. There is no need for propaganda, for missionaries. Some will come; some will not. Sorrow and struggle may have led you to Zen, but however you come, it must be with a clear conscience and a pure heart. You must have a desperate desire to see life as it really is, and you must not permit anything to keep you from this, no matter how many blind alleys of religious creeds you may have stumbled into in the past. You may read all the books in all the libraries in the world; you may write thousands upon thousands of pages of your own opinions, but if your mind is not thoroughly clear, if your knowledge does not come from the real source, you will never know who you are. You will remain a stranger to your true self, a stranger to the naked truth.

21

Our Own Light

THE PRACTICE of Zen is nothing but the practice of sunyata, emptiness. Through our zazen, we realize a self that is pure and free. We are a great deal more than all the stories, bad and glad and sad, that we tell about ourselves. The real aim of our practice is to help us conduct our lives from this truth, to come from this place.

We are thinking beings. We must, in our everyday life, think a great deal. But we do not come to understand This Matter through thinking. What is thinking? Thinking is considering, weighing ideas, pondering this and that, back and forth. Not thinking is simply the denial of thinking. But zazen is neither of these. Zazen is *without* thinking. This *without* goes beyond thinking or not thinking. It is accepting the presence of ideas without either affirming or denying them; sitting on the cushion with our minds vividly awake; allowing a thought to come in and allowing it to go, without praising it, without blaming it, without loving it, without getting caught in weighing and judging; just without thinking. It is the pure presence of things just as they are: in-breath; out-breath. Zazen is not a conscious effort to blank out one's mind, not by any means. Zazen is simply without any intentional attitude at all. There is no "I believe" or "I disbelieve." There is no affirming, no denying; no accepting, no rejecting. It is in this condition of being without thinking that we reach the ground of our being. This is the place from which all subsequent thinking and reflection comes. This is the strong seat, the firm foundation.

Dogen investigated the nature of zazen, and he came to believe that to understand the consciousness that we have in zazen is to understand consciousness in general. From the Buddhist point of view, the true nature of the mind is clear light. The illusions, the extra thoughts do not reside in the nature of the mind. They are temporary, and can be removed. We sit, simply, to remove all of these extra things. Fundamentally, the mind is an entity of clarity and light. We all have this mind; we are all Buddha from the beginning, without exception. But when we first begin to sit, it is hard for us to understand this, because we cover it over with all our conceptualizing: Is it this or is it that, am I right or am I wrong, what am I spending seven days sitting on the cushion for, this is crazy, and so on—all kinds of thoughts.

If we can stop our conceptualizing and just let our minds rest in their natural state, we may experience something wonderful. But to trust this is very hard. To trust this, it is necessary to go back to the condition we were in before we first began putting some kind of dimmer, or filter, on our experiences. We need to be able to experience this moment just as it is, where we are, right here. And we need to keep the mind flexible, open to whatever comes.

Zen practice must have that flexibility. Yes, we ask that everyone sit still, that everyone be punctual and silent and do everything to make the atmosphere as clear as possible. But if someone needs to sit in a chair, or lie on the floor, if there is some adaptation that must be made for our Western backgrounds, then we must respond, for we are not glued to the rules of the past. We must know our tradition, where we have come from, but be ready to move on.

Any experience that we have had we can later analyze and ponder, but while we are living it, we must be in it. The great baseball player *is* the baseball when he hits it; the thought of hitting the ball is an impediment to playing. Having been through repeated practice, he has developed a technical mastery; he performs best when not thinking about it at all, but he has this strong background. The same is true of zazen. There can be no separation between you and it, no thought of doing well or doing badly. Sitting after sitting, with this strong discipline, our practice deepens. Our bodies become stronger, our minds become clearer, our reactions to events become faster, freer, more spontaneous, so that when we are up at bat, we just hit the ball, without a single thought of whether or not we can do it, or whether or not we'll fail. The true life of our Zen practice comes from sitting quietly, doing nothing, and then getting up quietly and acting dynamically and directly in our everyday lives.

We learn a great deal about the intuitive wisdom of our bodies when we sit. There is a power that lies in nonresistance, and this is the real meaning of being at attention without tension. You know that in winter, the tree boughs that bend under the snow survive, while the ones that resist break. So in your pain, don't resist; bend. Go with it, breathe with it, let your body teach you, let it tell you what it means. Nothing is fixed. The stillness that we have in the zendo is wonderful, but the real stillness is the stillness in movement; then the true rhythm can be understood. There are many ways this true rhythm can be expressed, many ways of using this wonderful energy that comes from letting go. When the ever-intrusive ego gets out of the way, then the hitter, the bat, and the ball; the archer, the bow, and the arrow; the pianist, the instrument, and the music are one. We don't play; it plays us. We don't breathe; it breathes us.

We become stiller and stiller through our sitting. We didn't first prepare a condition of stillness and then sit. We are lucky to come to a house that is already full of good vibrations. But the stillness, the good vibes, are created by our own sitting. In this stillness, in the deep silence of the zendo, the border between inner and outer, motion and rest is dissolved. There is no gate: all gates are open. The 84,000 pores of our skin are breathing, and we are finding that the breathing, and our complete absorption in it, lengthens and deepens all by itself. Just being present with what is happening, we forget ourselves; we are absorbed in just being.

"Everybody has his own light," Ummon told his assembled monks. "If he tries to see it, everything is darkness." Every person has his or her own light. This sounds like what is known as self-power, which is associated with the Zen way. Jodo Shinshu [Shin Buddhism, "True School of the Pure Land"] is based on so-called other-power. Jodo Shinshu practitioners recite the name of Amida Buddha over and over and over: Namu Amidabu, Namu Amidabu, Namu Amidabu. I have given this practice to some of you, and I do it myself. It's a wonderful practice, uniting with Amida Butsu. ["Butsu," or the abbreviation "Bu," is Japanese for Buddha. "Amida" stands for both life and light.]

But is there really any contradiction between self-power and other-power? When the self thinks too much of itself and schemes to achieve self-liberation, this is quite unproductive. When this scheming is put aside, there is no need to say there is a gap between self-power and other-power. The self and other are never separate. The self had nothing to do from the very beginning. Everything is due to the other. We do not do this by ourselves. There is simply the in-breath . . . the out-breath . . . giving . . . receiving . . . opening. Zazen is opening to the whole universe, not just to ourselves, but to God, or Tao, or whatever. That is what we are here to experience.

When Soen Roshi was in Israel one spring he wrote this wonderful haiku:

Crawling out of the Dead Sea
body glittering
with drops of spring.

Crawling out from the Dead Sea, spring drops glittering over
our bodies—that's what we are doing here. We are crawling out
of the Dead Sea. We are not just here to eat and excrete. We are
here to find out who we are, where we come from. What are
we living for? What is this all about? Some people are breathing, but they are not alive. They are in a dead condition. Quite
healthy people, in fact, due to some dulling circumstances in
their lives, can be half-alive, partly dead. So we are here to wake
up. Attending sesshin, we are crawling out of the Dead Sea and
seeing some glittering light in us and around us. No matter how
cloudy the day, that light is always glittering. Crawling out of
the Dead Sea—in sesshin, we go one step further: we die on the
cushion, not just in the Dead Sea.

Die on the cushion. Give it all up. Die to all the pettiness, all
the nastiness, all the self-preoccupation, all the self-pity, all this
stuff. And then be resurrected; really live. Then see spring
come, sparkling and fresh.

In the spring season, we think about Buddha and his birthday, Christ and Easter, Passover, the vernal equinox. All these
things are wonderful celebrations at this time of year. Buddha
and Christ were human beings who gave up everything, gave it
up at the age of thirty and practiced very strong ascetic discipline. Buddha sat, sat, sat; experienced enlightenment; gave his
first sermon; and taught for forty-five years.

Christ, after three years of being in the wilderness, died. It
was only a short period of time to teach. But during that period
he gave wonderful, important teaching to all of us: the teaching
of love and forgiveness. He was betrayed. He was despised. He
was rejected. He died on the cross and his most important teaching was "Forgive them, for they know not what they do." Love,
in spite of everything. Forgive, no matter what. When he died,

his last words were said to have been, "My God, my God, why hast Thou forsaken me?" And this is a great mystery to some people. Did God forsake him? In the opinion of Dom Aelred Graham, the great Catholic theologian, it was "my" God that had forsaken Jesus—the God he had always thought about in his human mind. That God had vanished, not the ultimate one. But as Ummon said, if we try to see this, it is all darkness.

"What is everybody's light?" asked Ummon. Nobody said a word, so Ummon answered. He was very fond of giving the answer. Everybody's light is "the hall and the gate," right here under our noses. There are many ways to express this. Ummon's way is clear, direct, poetic. This hall, this cushion, this floor— each thing contains everything. Take it as it is.

Our ego sets itself up against others, making judgments, contradicting, conflicting, striving, asserting. We say, "This is my way; you have to do it my way." Of course, we all must have some feeling about what we are doing in this world. We shouldn't just sit back and be blobs! You understand that, of course. But you also understand that in deep zazen, in deep practice, all of this melts down. Out of that melting down, real compassion is born. And out of that compassion, we can *do* something.

22

Time Unfolds

Nᴏᴛ ʀᴇsɪsᴛɪɴɢ, we breathe in the sound of the rain, of the birds, of the gong, of our feet as we walk on this wonderful squeaky floor—not resisting, we breathe these sounds in, we breathe them out. We dissolve into them, and they into us. This is listening practice, just being present with each sound, whatever it is: cars passing by, a fire engine zooming along making a terrific noise, every kind of sound. Nothing is a disturbance, nothing is an intrusion.

To sit together for five days of intensive practice, to live together, to work together in silence: this is an ancient tradition. All of us have different reasons for having begun to sit on the cushion. What I hear from most people is that they have come because of deep pain, or loneliness, or restlessness, or some feeling that something is lacking. But as the days go by, the pain and loneliness give way to feelings of belonging in this universe, feeling supported by all the people who are here together and who are in other places as well—supported by the universal Sangha. The restlessness subsides. The silence and the stillness of our posture; the breath being allowed to flow; all of this contributes to our stability, our rootedness. With each breath, with each step in kinhin, we feel our connectedness to this earth on which we live, and to one another. This sense of composure and silent communication is right in the walls of this house, in the floors, in every part of it: "upstairs, downstairs, and in my lady's chamber." We come in and we don't have to create any of this; it's right here. Everybody steps right into it and settles down immediately.

We are practicing this ancient tradition authentically. We come here to live a simple and straightforward life together. What we are studying is This Mind, and for this we must be very direct, very honest with ourselves. Accepting every situation just as it is, just saying yes to it; neither approving nor rejecting it; this helps us to accept quietly what the ego would instantly and automatically thrust away. Instead of saying, "I don't want that, I don't want to hear that, I don't want to experience that," we let it all come in, just the way we listen to all the sounds occurring from moment to moment. Then we are lifted out of our little ego-selves, free to live and act from wholeness.

This is a practice of seeing into ourselves, realizing we have no fixed form. Clearly experiencing the ground of our being, we realize its imperturbability no matter what happens. We have this wonderful core. If we really experience this, sitting after sitting after sitting, whatever we do becomes zazen, and we are one with whatever confronts us. When reading, we read. When walking, we walk. When eating, we eat, and so on. One act! One deed! One whole and true experience.

Where do we practice? Everywhere! On the street, in the kitchen, everywhere. But from time to time, we come to a special place of practice, such as this house on Sparks Street, and we have so-called formal practice. This gives us a wonderful framework, a good design, a base. And then we return to every other activity, and experience more deeply that every other activity is itself the practice of the Dharma. Experiencing this simple and direct mind shows us that everything is the practice of the Dharma.

Somebody came to me once after visiting a certain place and said she didn't like it very much because there wasn't a lot of Dharma there. But what was she talking about? There is nothing but Dharma in the whole universe. If she wasn't clued into it where she was, that's not the Dharma's fault. The wonderful order of the universe itself is the manifestation of Dharma. Buddhahood is right on this earth. The lotus grows in the mud, in the night; to understand this is really to experience zazen.

The first rule of zazen, handed down from generation to generation, is to have compassion for all beings, and a deep longing to save all of them. We must practice samadhi meditation with great care, promising to ferry all sentient beings over to the other shore. We refuse to practice zazen only for our own emancipation. At the end of each of our activities together, we chant the Four Great Vows, beginning with the vow to save all sentient beings. This vow is based on the fact that we are one with all beings.

When we take our meals together, we chant the verse of the three morsels. The first morsel is to destroy all evils. As we take this first morsel, or offer this first morsel, we cut off all our delusive thoughts. This is where the evil begins—with us. We don't say that there is a lot of evil in the world and we have to offer this morsel to destroy it. It's to destroy all these egocentric things in our own being that we are here.

The second morsel is to practice all good deeds. We do this inconspicuously. We take this practice with us into whatever we are doing, never thinking for a moment, "I am doing a good deed"; never expecting any praise for it, just doing.

The third morsel is to save all sentient beings. This is like the beginning of the Four Great Vows. When we vow to save all sentient beings, *we* cannot do it, but by offering ourselves to the Dharma, throwing ourselves away, giving up our egocentric thoughts that *we* are doing something, then we may be able to help one another on this planet.

The tradition in Zen temples is to eat as quickly as possible, so that the monks can get back to zazen as quickly as possible. The assumption is that they are so enamoured with zazen that they do not want to leave it for one minute longer than necessary. So eating is usually done quickly, neatly, and clearly. And the tradition is also to eat one-third less than one might like. Now, since Zen practice is to be flexible, not to adhere to fixed patterns, if for some reason you would like to eat more slowly, or you need to take more food, please, by all means, do so. Nobody here is forcing you to do anything against your nature. Those of us who have finished will sit and do the zazen that we are enamoured of.

Our zazen practice is the most direct way to the truth of Buddhism. We don't have many lectures here, we don't have any big discussions, we don't sit around after sesshin and comment on our experiences. Instead of wandering about conceptualizing, we sit with our whole being, not just our intellect. In one of the sutras it says, "Let your mind concentrate in silence, and let it remain motionless like Mt. Sumeru. If you practice in this way you are already in the world of the Buddhas while among sentient beings." This is called "the direct entrance into the Buddha-world in one jump." This is why Zen Buddhism is called the teaching of sudden awareness. It is for this awareness that we practice zazen. The intellectual stuff has its place in the world, but not in our zazen. We just give our bare, clear attention to the various happenings of the day as they come up, letting go of all our habits, all our interference. In this way, our minds become healthier. In accepting our pain, our discomfort, and our frustration, rather than trying to repress or avoid any of it, we come upon true ego strength, egoless ego strength. It is important to allow changes in ourselves in every way. There is no fixed zazen posture; the body may want to give a little here or there. The breath may want to change its rhythm. We may want to let a whole lot fall off. It is essential to permit these changes in ourselves. We have no fixed form.

Rain is falling; snowflakes are falling; the sun is shining. Everything is happening right now, at this moment. To talk about it is easy, but to really experience it—this is why we sit, sit, sit. We are told, "You have Buddha-nature from the very beginning, so what is there to do?" But unless we know this from the depths of our hearts, through our strong, disciplined zazen, we cannot express it in our lives. Each one of us must have our own experience. No one else's experience can be superimposed on ours. We are led astray by our egocentric thinking, our dwelling on "me." Of course, our ordinary consciousness has to be involved with what we need to do, what we should wear, where we are going, what food we should eat, where we should live, and so on. But here, during these days of just sitting, we drop all of that. Here, we have everything we need right at this moment. And when we go back to our everyday lives, perhaps we will see more clearly the things we can let go of there, too. Perhaps we don't need quite so much, quite so many things. Perhaps we can be less grabby. Having changed our attitude a little bit after sitting, sitting, sitting, we are able to see more clearly what our life is about.

There is no final realization. In this no-knowing, wondering-on, openhearted condition of mind, we face directly whatever comes—good, bad, ugly, beautiful. We don't push anything under the rug, we don't buffer it with something; we experience it fully. Just listening . . . when somebody strikes the gong, becoming one with that sound, not reflecting, "Oh, that's the sound of the gong," but just being that sound. No separation; nothing but gong, nothing but this very moment.

Western as well as Eastern philosophers have inquired a great deal about time. This moment, that moment, past, present, future. David Hume, a Western philosopher, said that whenever we have no successive perceptions, we have no notion of time. He said, "Time cannot make its appearance to the mind either alone or attended by a steady, unchangeable object; it is always discovered by some perceivable succession of changeable objects." Hume is on the very edge of Zen insight. He is saying that the idea of time is a product of change, and change can only occur when there is more than one object, or at least more than one quality. So we may presume that when there are no objects, there is no time. Time was invented with naming. Separation occurs when one thing is set apart from another, through naming. However much we may try to divide and classify the world by means of words, it is still one; it is never really divided. As soon as one thing is named, however, everything else seems to exist in relation to it. That creates an inescapable duality. Before such definitions are made, nothing stands in relationship to, or apart from, anything else. There is no knower, no known; there are no subjects and no objects, no succession of objects and therefore no time.

A Western philosopher might say, from things we get words. In the Zen view, from words we get things. All that we actually experience is in the immediate present—Now—and we can never experience anything beyond this Now. There has never been anything other than this Now, this moment. No matter how many periods of time, even tens of thousands of them, that we can think of, they consist of nothing but the present moment, the absolute Now. All existence, all worlds are realized in each temporal particularity.

Raindrops, fluttering snowflakes, mists—nothing is separate from this moment. And of course, we do not deny the seeming succession of temporal moments—it is necessary to be punctual in the zendo—but once we sit down, we forget about it. When our sitting is really deep and strong, we say, time flies by. Time unfolds. Before we know it, the bell has rung. Living each moment fully, each sitting fully, each kinhin Now, time loses its grip. With this quality of attention, the little ego vanishes. Having gone beyond time, we are freely present to each moment.

Our true action is our action without acting. We are so completely present with whatever it is that we have no thought of acting. We are so completely in zazen that we cannot possibly say we are doing zazen.

23

Listening to the Mind

THE MIND IS not an individual matter; it does not belong
to our egocentric consciousness. The more we give up that
egocentric consciousness, the more we experience the mind as
free and joyful. Through our zazen practice, all the junk gets
swept away; we feel the Dharma light shining everywhere. The
universal wakefulness that is in every one of us shows itself
more clearly every minute.

Somebody told me about hearing an extraordinary musical
performance, and wondered if this was Buddha-mind. Now this
may be an expression of Buddha-mind, but it is not Buddha-
mind. What is Buddha-mind? Buddha-mind is with us every
single breath. How we express this Buddha-mind is another
story. Buddha-mind is not some *thing*. It is not a mirror, it is
not a tree, it is not this or that.* What is it? We are here to
experience this mind, and then we show it, in our ordinary lives,
in musical performances, in cooking, in cleaning, in whatever

---

*A reference to the verses of Shen-hsiu and Hui-neng, the Sixth Patriarch.
Shen-hsiu's verse stressed "polishing the mirror" of the mind so that no
dust obscured its clarity; in his verse, Hui-neng declared, "Buddha-nature
is always clean and pure. Where is there room for dust?"

way. We show it in being a mother, a father, a friend, a lover—whatever. Yo-Yo Ma plays the Bach *Suites for Unaccompanied Cello* in a way that is a spiritual treasure. Anyone who listens cannot help but feel that this is Buddha-mind expressing itself. He may not know anything about Buddhism, but his Buddha-mind is shining through. It's a completely selfless kind of music-making, completely giving up to the true spirituality of Bach, who was a deeply spiritual man.

Sesshin is a time in which we can experience this Buddha-mind condition very deeply. There is a lightness, a deep, joyful spirit. We feel this by opening our hearts. We open up, completely, letting our 84,000 pores breathe this in. It's a treasure. When sesshin is over and we go back to whatever our lives are, we go back with a feeling of a deep bond to one another, without ever having said a word. This bond is not one of attachment or dependence. We don't think, "I can't sit without those wonderful people around me." It's quite a different story. It's a sense that we have all experienced something marvelous together—again, without saying a word. We have been working together, eating together, doing all these things in a harmonious condition that is truly a treasure.

One of our Sangha members came to me and said she was going away for a few months. "What shall I do? How shall I support my practice?" she asked me. "I am going to Europe, and will be living in hotel rooms, and I don't know how I will carry on." I said, "Sit down and take a deep breath, and you will be right here. We are together wherever we are, when we just sit down and take a deep breath."

We are all supporting each other wherever we are in the world, without saying, "Let me do this for you, you poor thing, how will you get along without us"—no, no. Just by being present. And as I've said many times, your zazen is your best teacher. Zazen washes away all conceptual thought, and makes the mind clear and fresh. You all have your own zazen mind, so listen to it. Your zazen mind teaches you about just how far you are going, just how much you trust, just how willing you are to believe in this mind, just how clearly you are coming to understand with your bones, your skin, your marrow, what this is about.

Through your zazen, you are giving up your discriminating attitudes and becoming absolutely clear and still. Sometimes you experience great pain, yet you remain sitting, sitting, sitting, not giving up; awake to everything. Sometimes it's noisy outside: chainsaws, children playing, people laughing and talking. It's all O.K., because you're awake to everything, to every single thing. If somebody makes a noise in the zendo, it's O.K. If somebody cries, it's fine. Cars go by and beep: no problem. Planes fly overhead: fine. Cats meow, dogs bark: good. Nothing is a disturbance when your zazen condition has become firm and clear. All judgmental attitudes about whether or not those noises are disturbing simply fall away.

It's one thing to sit in ideal conditions in the zendo, but we need to be ready to sit anywhere, on the streetcar, on the bus, anywhere! The world goes on, the sounds go on, the raindrops fall, the wind blows, and we are learning all this acceptance of it through our bodies, which sit still no matter what. If you want to memorize things in books about how to practice, fine, but it's not the same, is it. You don't read the menu to taste the food.

During sesshin, someone may ask me, "Why am I doing this? Why am I going through so much pain? Isn't there some easier way?" But at the end of sesshin, that same person may say to me, "Well, I understand now. It feels good; in fact, it feels wonderful. So I will go through it again and again and again."

We cannot wait for some other time to experience this. Today is a wonderful day. Today is a fresh day. Sitting in a posture that is strong and grounded, with a mind that is still and composed, not dead but dynamically composed, buoyant and joyful, we maintain this condition without any pressure, without any pushing, without any gaining idea.

Engo said, "To guard and maintain the essential teachings of

Buddhism must be the vocation of the noble soul." To guard and maintain the essential teachings of Buddhism we are here, sitting, going directly to what needs to be done. We are cutting off all extraneous matters; no blinking, no hesitation, going straight ahead. Who is the noble soul? Who is this person without rank? Forget about it. Forget about seeking Buddha, forget about words, forget about this outside self. The true person without rank, the noble soul, is within us. There is no noble soul without. Only when we experience it in this way in our own words and lives, do the vivid words and actions of our ancestral teachers come forth.

Someone came and said to me, "It makes me very happy to discover that all those ancient teachers' words are, after all, true." Indeed. Become the person of no rank. Become the noble soul, and live in this awakened way, not imitating anyone. Whatever the circumstances your life asks of you, respond to them in your own individual Zen spirited way. Don't waste any time trying to be someone else—certainly not someone who lived in the ninth century in some other culture. We are not here to have someone else's experience. We are here to have our own vivid experience. So please don't cling to yesterday, to what happened, to what didn't happen. And do not judge today by yesterday. Let us just live today to the fullest! Moment after moment, each sitting is the only sitting.

24

True Seeing

FUNYOMITTA TOLD his teacher Bashashita that he wanted to become a monk. Bashashita asked him what he would do as a monk. "Nothing special," Funyomitta said.

His teacher then asked, "What will you not do?" Funyomitta replied, "Secular affairs." Bashashita asked again, "What *will* you do?" Funyomitta said, "Sacred affairs." His teacher questioned him further: "What do you mean by 'sacred affairs'?" Funyomitta answered, "When I am tired, I sleep. When I am thirsty, I drink." Bashashita said, "You already have true wisdom. I am sure that your renunciation will be extremely meritorious, and I now ordain you as a true monk."

The word "monk" comes from the Greek word "monos," which means one. To become a monk means to become one. Asked what he would do as a monk, Funyomitta didn't say, "I suppose I will polish my practice," or "I will help people." He did not say "I" at all. This true monk said, "Nothing special." Having already experienced this understanding of what it is to be a monk, he could not do anything special. The Dharma was working through him. There was no need to say "*I* will do this, *I* will do that."

When we look at the universe as this "monos," this oneness, instead of something compartmentalized, we see the mysterious fact that death, health, and illness are one. The true face of the universe includes good, bad, life, death, health, illness—all of it.

Here we are, in this beautiful place, Green Gulch Farm. Whenever anyone in Massachusetts asks about it, I say it's paradise. Everything is so lovingly cared for—all the trees, flowers, and even the stones seem to have special attention from each of you. This loving care is what greets me when I come here. Outside the zendo, there is a tree that still has fruit. And next to it is another tree that is flowering for the next fruit. This is such a wonderful teaching, right here. Just to be in this atmosphere is refreshing and clarifying and healing.

In the verse that accompanies the story about Funyomitta there is a question: "The desert of true nature does not grow the grasses of secular and sacred. Ten thousand vast miles, and not a plant to be seen. What flowers and leaves do you grow in your garden?" What flowers and leaves do we grow in our gardens? In other words, what is the scenery in our minds? Are we seeing things as they really are, without egocentric preoccupations and fixed points of view blocking our vision? Are we able to taste things fully, just being present with them moment after moment, just as they are? If we can let go of our egocentric stuff and just be present with what is here, we experience something extraordinary. The finite becomes infinite. And we take this with us, wherever we go. The flowers and trees in the gardens of our minds are purified by this experience. We do not need to talk about it; we do not need to describe it; above all, we do not need to analyze it. The point is to bring this experience into our lives; to live it.

There is a wonderful Zen saying: "Before I began Zen practice, mountains were mountains, rivers were rivers. When I had some experience, some more intimate understanding, I saw that mountains were not mountains; rivers were not rivers. Now that

I have come to the very substance and am at rest, I see that mountains are mountains; rivers are rivers."

In our neurotic compulsion to think, think, think, we interfere with our true seeing. For example, when we are going to meet someone, our minds are full of all kinds of unnecessary questions: Will this person like me? Will he not like me? Will it be a good thing for me to meet her? Will she like the way I dress? Will he approve of what I say? With such preoccupations, we completely miss the reality of the person we meet. The face, the name, the interests of that person may be entirely lost because we are so full of ourselves. Once a friend of mine was about to go to Italy. I asked her if she had been there before. "Yes," she said, "but I didn't see it. I was too full of myself. So I'm going back, and this time, I hope to see it."

We come to Zen practice to change this kind of preoccupied way of living, to let go of such attitudes, such fears about how we present ourselves, how we might be perceived, whether something will be good for us or not. Through this practice, we come to a condition in which we truly believe that our Buddha-nature will meet the Buddha-nature in the other person.

We are all so afraid of change, afraid of death, afraid of uncertainty. We are sometimes even afraid of getting well. How many of us have chosen boredom and suffering over the uncertainty of change! We have chosen to remain stuck with what we know, even though what we don't know may be so much more wonderful. Yet in spite of this kind of attitude, everything is always changing. It is just our egocentric minds that are trying to hold things in some unchanging place, trying to keep what we think of as good conditions and trying to eliminate so-called bad conditions; and in the process, we become greedy and angry, because nothing remains the same.

How does our Zen training help us change? So simply. It helps us do what needs to be done, whether it's cleaning, sitting, sleeping, or eating. When we are completely engaged in our activities, we are creating some stability within the ever-

changing world in which we live. There is a feeling of being
rooted in this simple practice. We are no longer pulled here and
there in a tug-of-war. We sit, and in our sitting, we experience
the eternal, this Buddha-mind, or Buddha-nature, or whatever
we want to call it, within the changing scenery. And through
our practice, we maintain this mind as a presence in our lives,
no matter what happens—storms, disappointments, illnesses—
whatever happens, we find nourishment and stability. We are
ready to face whatever it is clearly.

Last summer, when I was going through some slight indisposition in my life, many of you wrote to me and sent me your
loving wishes. A beautiful card was made here at Green Gulch,
with messages from many of you. When I received it, I sat down
in my living room and cried, not in sadness, but in deep gratitude that such friends are here, and that such loving support is
in my life. I kept that card, and I read it every so often. I smile,
and say again, "Thank you, thank you; thank you even to those
who seemed to think I was not going to live much longer."

As you can see, I am really extremely well, and do intend to
live a good deal longer. But even if that doesn't happen, the
quality of my life is very good, thanks to your loving support.
Some people tell me that I am denying my illness. "Why don't
you face it?" they ask. But I am not sick; I have not been sick,
in the sense of having any symptoms or pain, except from what
is normally caused by a major operation. This indisposition was
discovered through an annual checkup; there was no warning
that anything was wrong. So having discovered this, all kinds
of tests were done, punctures, incisions, excisions—you name it,
I had it. The doctors have been very perplexed, because I have
not had any pain, or any fevers, or anything else on their list. I
have been a very difficult patient, in that I don't fit into a prescribed cubbyhole.

I do face the fact of what has been going on, and I share it
with you because there are changes in my body that may give
me trouble at some time. But the doctors have told me, "Since

you aren't feeling sick, we won't give you any treatments that will make you sick. Go home and use your own mind for all of this. That's the treatment for you." Perhaps they have done a little zazen themselves at some point! So let us be joyful together; let us be whole and well in this life, at this moment. Like Funyomitta, we do not do anything special. When we are tired, we sleep; when we are thirsty, we drink.

25

One Act

WHEN SOMEONE asks you about Zen, what do you do? I hope you don't deliver a lecture on Buddhism. I hope you don't even say one word, but instead just show by the kind of life that you are living that this is a wonderful and inspiring and extraordinarily simple practice, and that it is the *practice* that is essential—not talking about it, but doing it. Somebody told me about the latest translation of the *Tao Te Ching,* calling it "a wonderful distillation of what happens when you've been sitting for many, many years." I said, "This is not an expression of sitting for many, many years at all. Sitting for many, many years? There is no word to be said. Not one." Words are not it. "It has no form, much less a name," as Daio Kokushi said.

Why do we sit for hours on end? Why do we endure pain, weariness, all the rest of it? Master Gutei asked himself these same questions in his youth. In an effort to find out, he went to live all by himself in a hermitage. He sat as we sit. He chanted as we chant. He prepared his food, just as we do. Days went by; his sesshin was endless. It was a quiet way to live, a good place for zazen, and Gutei was enjoying it. Of course, there was no challenge to what he was doing. Then one day a figure appeared out of the twilight and silently walked toward the hut. A nun had arrived on the scene, dressed in the clothes of a traveling priest, with a broad straw hat, a black robe, straw sandals, and a staff. She walked around Gutei three times, threw her staff down on the ground, and said, "Speak! Speak! Say something, and I will take off my hat." Now this was a real challenge— Dharma combat. Let's see what your understanding of Zen is, she was saying to Gutei.

Poor Gutei. He was not really prepared for visitors. He had nothing to say. It wasn't that he had nothing to say out of profound, deep understanding, but just that he was really puzzled, really caught off guard. The nun walked around him once more, giving him another chance, and again she challenged him, "Speak! Speak!"

Three times she did this. She was very generous, giving him plenty of time to collect himself. But still, he had nothing to say; nothing to show. All kinds of thoughts started up in his head: What does three mean? Why is she doing this? What can I say to this? And so on. The more he thought about it, the more confused he got. Well, he thought, I'll need a little more time. So he said, "It's already dark outside. Please stay overnight." The nun replied, "Say a word, and I'll stay." Gutei did not know what to reply. So the nun walked out into the night, and that was it. That night, Gutei was really troubled. What a stupid fool I am, he thought. Have you heard that phrase from yourself to yourself? What a stupid person I am? This is useless, of course; it's a great waste of time, but we all do it. Finally Gutei told himself, This will not do. I must set out in search of somebody who can give me some inkling of what this is about, of what's wrong with my practice.

This was a good moment for him. What's wrong? What needs some attention? What is this about? Why am I doing this? What are we doing sitting here? Speak, speak! Zen practice is not about being numb, not about just going through the motions. Gutei had been sitting, chanting, eating, sleeping, cleaning; but where was the spirit of Zen? Where was the life, the fire? Where was the living, dynamic response to something new and different?

That night, Gutei had a dream in which the Bodhisattva Kannon said, "Do not leave this mountain. Stay where you are, because a living bodhisattva is coming to visit you, and you will have the instruction you need." So Gutei waited, as patiently as he could. And sure enough, a few days later along came Tenryu. Gutei told him his whole sad story, and said how perturbed he was about his practice. He asked Tenryu, "What is the essence of Buddhist teaching? Please tell me." We hear this in so many Zen stories. Please tell me. Please teach me. Please show me how to do this. What's the secret? There must be some secret you're holding back from me. Please give it to me.

So what did Tenryu do? He didn't deliver a long lecture on the essence of Buddhist teaching. He didn't tell Gutei what he should do. He just sat down beside Gutei, and he *sat* with him. He was not sitting there dozing off, nor was his mind somewhere else. He was *sitting* with Gutei. He was *present* with Gutei. This was his teaching. This is *the* teaching. And then, at the crucial moment, he looked at Gutei, and he held up his finger, and suddenly, Gutei understood. It was the right moment. What does this mean, this one finger? I have read this koan many, many times, and I have given talks about it many times, but every time it's different. Every time, something in it strikes me a little bit differently. I was sitting with it this morning, seeing that scene in which Tenryu sat with Gutei, really sat with Gutei, and then raised one finger.

Another story tells of Gutei's young attendant, who no doubt had heard this story. We all hear wonderful stories from our teachers, and their teachers, and their teachers' teachers. This student began to imitate his teacher. When asked about Gutei's teaching, he raised one finger. It was imitation; nothing real. It was not done from his own understanding, from his own expression. When Gutei heard about this, he called the student to him and cut off the young man's finger. At that moment the attendant suddenly understood. Now please remember that in these stories, "cutting off" is not to be taken literally. Perhaps it really happened, who knows? But this is symbolic: cutting off the student's attachment to the teacher, and cutting off any attachment to the idea that raising one finger was the teaching. The finger has nothing to do with it, so cut it off, get rid of it. In his commentary Mumon says, "The enlightenment of Gutei and of the boy does not depend on the finger. If you understand this, Tenryu, Gutei, the boy, and you yourself are all run through with one skewer."

One finger does have something to do with it. When Gutei raised one finger, it was with *one* mind, *one* act. This *one* is the key word. In "The Song of Zazen," Hakuin said, "Even those who have practiced it for just one sitting will see all their evil karma erased." But one sitting doesn't mean one forty-five-minute period. It means a sitting which is all-embracing, a sitting for all sentient beings, a sitting with and for one another. *One* sitting; *one* finger; and then expressing it. How do we express this *one?* Everyone has his or her own name for it, but the experience of it is what we are here for, not the naming of it. How do we express it in our lives? What are we doing here? Why are we engaged in this life practice?

We are not sitting here for our own salvation. This practice is not for your salvation or my salvation. We are sitting here together for the sake of all sentient beings. Sometimes, at the end of the day, instead of chanting the Four Great Vows we say, "May we extend This Mind over the whole universe, so that we and all beings together may attain maturity in Buddha's wisdom." *This* Mind, this *one* mind, we are extending over the whole universe. Even if we're tired, we take another deep breath and go on. Even if we don't feel like coming to the zendo, we come, because we have promised that we will, and people are counting on us.

Not long ago, somebody came to me and said, "I can't come

to sesshin because there's some family matter that I have to take care of; anyway, I can sit on a cushion anywhere. I can sit down and just breathe at home." That's perfectly true. We can sit down on a cushion and breathe anywhere. But we're not doing this just anywhere, or just for ourselves. We attend sesshin to support and offer ourselves to others in this practice. And when we do this with and for one another, it's quite a different experience. We feel the effects of everyone's sitting. There is a clear, powerful atmosphere. Everybody who participates and extends this mind helps make this wonderful stillness palpable. We maintain silence during sesshin so we can feel this, breath after breath, step after step. We maintain this stillness, and we sense something that we could not have realized otherwise.

Gutei's cutting off his student's finger has yet another meaning for us. We all know that when we have some deep pain, whether from slicing off a finger or from some serious illness or from something else, we feel what really matters. If we confront that deep pain, feel that pain, it clears out a lot of stuff. It makes us stop and consider what is really important. The other day, one of my doctors said to me, "When a glass of milk falls and breaks, you don't worry about the spilled milk; you pick up the pieces of glass so they don't hurt anybody." So don't worry over spilled milk. Feel something cleared away by that pain. What is essential? What really matters? What are we doing here?

Sitting like this together, what is your life expression of this, your immediate expression of this? Don't copy mine; don't copy someone else's. What is your clear Zen expression, your unselfconscious expression? If a nun walks into your sitting place and says "Speak! Speak!", what will you say? What will you do? How will you show it in your life? Gutei always raised his finger, but it was never the same. It was always fresh, always new. Every day we sit, but it's never the same. We take this wonderful posture, we regulate our breath, we pay attention to it, and it's never the same. Every sitting is different. There are no repetitions. The conditions are a little bit different, the atmosphere slightly changed. Everything is always moving on. Nothing is static; it is always fresh and clear. Gutei said, "I have practiced this one-finger Zen my whole life, and it has never become exhausted." This one-pointed mind, this all-embracing mind is never exhausted. All we have to do is tune in, and that's what we are here to do.

"Speak! Speak!" doesn't mean that I want you to tell me something at dokusan. "Speak! Speak!" means, how do you respond to your life? Maybe it is necessary to speak sometimes. Maybe it's necessary to do all kinds of things. But whatever the response, it must be one that comes from an unself-conscious, freed-up, open, spacious mind. The revelation of our own wonderful human reality comes through the exploration of our own mind, and the intuitive realization of how we get in the way. Our practice is to help us get out of the way—to let go of all our hang-ups.

We hang on to the things that make us unhappy, and worry about things that we really cannot change. All that we can change is to allow this wonderful intuitive wisdom to work through us. All that we can do is to open up enough, to let go of all these things that worry and confuse us, and realize that there is deep happiness in the midst of all this tortured world— really deep happiness and joy. So please, let go of all your hang-ups. Don't worry; be happy. To be deeply grateful for this time together, deeply grateful for each stage of our lives; this really makes us quite happy. So let us continue, and continue, and continue.

26

Not Yet

"WHERE ARE YOU FROM?" is a classic Zen question. The way we answer says a lot about our condition of mind. Once a Zen master named Kyozan asked a monk this question. The monk said he had just been to Mount Rozan. Kyozan asked him if he had ever visited Goroho Peak. When the monk said he had not yet done so, Kyozan said, "You have not been to Mount Rozan." Rozan was the seat of Buddhist learning in China at that time. It had many beautiful temples and exquisite mountains, including the famed Mount Rozan, with its five peaks that were shaped like old men greeting one another, of which Goroho Peak was one. Here, of course, Kyozan was using Goroho Peak as a metaphor for spiritual realization. He was inquiring whether the monk had some insight into this matter of Zen. "Have you visited that peak?" "Not yet, not yet."

It is to be hoped that we all feel this way. This subtle matter is always just out of reach. We are always wondering on, more and more. Not yet, not yet. This great master was gently saying, in effect, "If you have not had a glimpse of that peak, then your condition is not yet ripe. Go ahead. Dig more deeply." This is a gentle way to teach. Each teacher has his or her own way. There can be no copycats, no imitators. Sometimes the same person will teach gently and sometimes give a shout, or sometimes a hit, depending on the circumstances. But all of this is to touch us most intimately. This Zen matter is most intimate. It is a matter of mind to mind; heart to heart.

We say that Zen cannot and should not be talked about, but then we go ahead and talk just the same, for the sake of opening up some doorway of understanding. And those of us who have to talk are aware of our responsibility; that what we say may have an effect that is encouraging or discouraging, confusing or clarifying. We must watch our steps closely. It's not a matter of just throwing some words out. Our hope is that in offering whatever little bit we have understood ourselves, the student's own inner eye will open. All our words, all our actions are for this. And we also know that it is not just our words, but everything around us that is delivering a teisho. The circumstances of the day, the work, each of you, everything and everyone is delivering the teaching.

True Zen insight is not *our* awareness. It does not belong to us. It is Buddha-mind awareness in us. *Just* Buddha-mind, or true person without rank, or whatever words we give it. The true person without rank was Rinzai's clear and direct way of referring to it. This true person without rank, this person deep within ourselves, let *this* person take over. This has nothing to do with time or space; it is not subject to circumstances. It has no name. The true person without rank works through us. All we have to do is let this come about. Our path is really pretty simple. It's just a quiet, endless walking on. But this path must be followed with our entire being, including all our good and bad baggage. We go along this way with deep concentration of body and mind. Our practice is continually refining itself so that in all situations, this Zen energy fills us up and manifests in everything we do. We do not need our judgments, our aversions, our negative attitudes to motivate us on this path. We need openheartedness.

Buddhism is not a set of doctrines. It has no dogma. It just teaches us about becoming buddhas. It is a way of spiritual self-development, but above all it is a way of action, first, last, and always. We must do something with this. We don't just sit around and talk about it, or sit on our cushions and gulp it all down for ourselves. We give it away; we radiate it. There are no shortcuts; there are no bypasses. There is no instant magical potion. We must go it on our own, on our two feet alone; yet we are always aware of our interrelatedness. Through each thought, each action, we can help or hinder one another. We take one step at a time, just as in kinhin. Just one step at a time. What we do will not be perfect, we know that. But, as R. H. Blyth says, "Perfection means not perfect actions in a perfect world, but appropriate actions in an imperfect one."

If we approach Zen practice with fixed ideas about what it will do for us, we just get in our own way. "Will this be good for me? Will it get me what I want? Is this what I'm here for? What if I have a wonderful enlightenment experience—will I look silly? What if I fail to have kensho and never understand anything all? How long will it take for me to come to some realization?" All these ideas are impediments. Why worry about satori? There are people of great Zen spirit and action who have never heard the word satori in their entire lives. There are people who have had satori who behave abysmally. Forget about enlightenment. If we have it, wonderful; we let it go, without a single thought about it. If we don't have it, fine; the accumulated practice of deep samadhi—intense, concentrated sitting, with no pushing, no forcing—penetrates our entire being. This is the most important thing. The path of Zen is not about experiencing some sudden burst of something that is gone in a flash. Having some insight, having kensho, is indeed wonderful, but then we let it go, and we don't talk about it, we don't discuss the experiences we have had with others. Such experiences are just the beginning, not the end of our practice. Even reading about other people's experiences can be a problem, because one can become attached to that description and think, "Oh, maybe it will happen to me that way." It can only happen as our experience, through our own zazen, in our own life. Then whatever it is we have experienced we give away to others, without saying a word about it. "See, I'm giving you my Zen. Isn't it wonderful?" No!

27

Forgetting
Everything

IN THE ANCIENT SUTRAS there are frequent references to training the wild ox. Perhaps an ox was used as a figure of speech because oxen were very precious in India. They still are—when I visited India, those huge, formidable, yet gentle creatures seemed to take over every scene.

The series of Oxherding Pictures used as a metaphor in Zen practice comes from this ancient tradition, and like so many metaphors, is a way of helping us to see a little bit more clearly how close our true home is to us. In the first picture of the Ten Oxherding Pictures, the verse reads in part, "Wild grasses grow green when the season comes; the flowers bloom in mad profusion day after day. Longing for home and yet not knowing how, tears flow and the kerchief is wet."

Throughout history, and even in our time, Zen has a tendency to be rather elitist. Many books make it seem as though it's only for people of a certain kind, only for those who can understand, who can do very strenuous discipline. Teachers throughout the ages have felt that this is a pity. I certainly feel it's a pity that the wonderful, essential practice of Zen should be denied somebody because he or she is not bright enough or not industrious enough or not something else enough.

We all have Buddha-nature from the very beginning, so there is nobody who can be excluded by being put in some cubbyhole, some category of deficiency. There are no exceptions. Everybody can taste this Buddha-nature, but sometimes—very often, in fact—we wonder about it. Does it really exist? In the first Ox-herding Picture, the person stands with a rope in hand and no ox in sight. This is a depiction of the way we often feel: I'm supposed to tame this wild ox-mind, but where is it? All I have is the rope to hold it with. I don't have anything to hold; I don't even know what it is I'm supposed to hold. I don't know what I'm supposed to tame. All I know is that I have come to this point, to this practice, because I feel there is something missing. I can't see it, I can't find it, I don't quite know what it is, but I know there is something missing; it is as though there is something I have forgotten, something that has become covered over by so many other things in my life. So now I have come to sit down quietly and let go of all these extraneous matters, to forget everything.

The highest state of mind is to have forgotten everything, according to a Mahayana text. This doesn't mean to have forgotten our true nature, but to have forgotten all the things that impede us from deeply experiencing it. It's like the story about the teacher entertaining an erudite guest. As is the custom, the teacher offered him a cup of tea, but when he began pouring, he didn't stop. The cup was overflowing, and the guest was in a state of real alarm that the room was soon going to be inundated with tea. "Please, please, stop," he said. "This cup is too full." The master said, "Yes, the cup is too full, and so, by the way, are you."

So it is with us. We need to empty out our concepts, our thoughts, our opinions about This Matter; we need to let it all go, to be completely open, as if this is the very first time we have ever sat. Indeed, every sitting is the first sitting. Then, what do we remember? We remember our connectedness to one another. We sense, without saying a single word, our common source. We feel how deeply the season of cold is upon us; how green the evergreens are against the snow. We smell the difference in the incense as it changes from day to day, we taste our food, we experience the feeling of the floor under our feet, the quality of our chanting. It's all fresh, beautiful, and alive.

When Kaji Nishitani was interviewed in an issue of *Parabola* magazine devoted to the topic of memory and forgetting, he was asked why we forget our true self, why we spend so much of our lives in forgetfulness. Or, as we might put it, why do we have to sit on the cushion over and over again? Professor Nishitani said that memory implies forgetting. We start from a recognition that there is something lacking, something forgotten; the question is, where does such a recognition come from? In Zen practice we have what is called the Great Doubt. This, Nishitani said, means that all knowledge, even philosophical knowledge, must be held in doubt. Great Doubt is a way of finding the truth, of forgetting in order to remember. The aim of such doubting is true, doubtless knowledge.

Each one of us sitting on our cushions has something essential to do with everyone else's true nature. Part of what we have forgotten is this: the nondifferentiation between self and the world. When we stop making separations between self and everything around us, we realize this one great Mind. And this is why we are here. Everything in the world is in our being right here, right now.

In this Zen practice of ours we must forget everything. When that forgetting is analyzed in a philosophical way; when we ask what there is to forget, what the true knowledge of our own nature is, we just entangle ourselves further. That kind of analysis is useless; give it up. We have to see, really see, from the state of forgetfulness. One of the most beautiful books in the Christian tradition is *The Cloud of Unknowing,* in which we are told that in order to be what one is meant to be, certain things must be forgotten; knowledge must be renounced. So it is for us: in order to experience this true nature, we must be willing to forget everything.

Here we are, rope in hand. Moment after moment, conditions are changing. Things clear up and become murky again. We get a glimpse of the ox; maybe the ox pulls on the rope; we pull back; there are all kinds of confrontations.

We see the tracks of the ox. Some are going east, some are going west; they start and then stop. The mind wanders off here, then wanders off there; it comes to some state of quietness and then wanders off again. The mind is still undisciplined, but we begin to see the tracks. We see that there is some place within us that is quiet, clear, uncluttered, peaceful, joyful in the midst of everything. What brings us to see this? Most often it comes from our own zazen. Sometimes it is something that we read—some Buddhist text or some wonderful piece of poetry— that touches us, that arouses something in us. We want to experience more of this. Many contemporary poets give us a glimpse. Zen itself is such a poetic practice.

Sometimes we meet a person who has some special kind of radiance that engages us. We wonder, where did that come from? How did this happen? Whenever I was with Soen Roshi I always felt how wonderful it was to be in such a joyful, luminous, almost childlike presence. And where did this come from? As we got to know him, we discovered that it was through a great struggle of his own that he came to have that quality. At one point, he contemplated suicide. Fortunately for us, he got out of that place, but some very dark things in his life brought him to his profound understanding. He had a deep realization of his own true nature, and then gave it away to everybody so spontaneously, so joyfully, so clearly.

Our engagement in this practice is enlightenment itself, nothing but. It is the process itself that is important. When we celebrate the enlightenment of the Buddha with Rohatsu sesshin, we are celebrating our own enlightenment from the very beginning. We are not waiting until December 8 so that we can look up at the morning star and suddenly have a great illumination. When the Buddha looked up at the star he realized that we are all, without exception, nothing but enlightened beings. Wonderful, wonderful! From the very beginning, every single being has this pure, clear, joyful Mind. He gave us the inspiration to realize This Mind. Our true enlightenment is just to see into this, to experience this peacefulness and to realize that the nature of This Mind is emptiness. There is no hanging on to anything.

Someone asked me, "Please tell me, how can I get a glimpse of my true nature?" Just let go of everything, everything. Let go of any preconceived notion of what you're going to get out of practicing Zen. Do not hold any ideas about Zen at all. It is not through ideas about your true nature but by experiencing it that you will know your original Mind. From the very beginning our minds are completely free from anything called sin; they are completely pure, completely without delusion, completely without suffering. Our true nature is pure, clear, and free. All kinds of things come up in our lives—hardships, pain, illness— but if we know our true nature, if we experience the bottom of our being, the ultimate ground of our being, none of these things can knock us over. There is no death. Of course we die, but there is the certainty in the midst of birth and death that we are living in the Great Time of eternity. There is no end to this. No matter that this body falls off, passes away; the joyful essence of life goes on.

So what do we remember, what do we forget? What about this matter of forgetting everything? Actually, we remember what is necessary for conducting our lives effectively. If we carried around all the other things that are not so necessary to remember, we would go crazy. Our intuitive minds make this distinction for us about what it is we need to remember and how much we can just let go of. While we are sitting in zazen, sitting in sesshin, we can let go of everything, absolutely everything. There's nothing we need to remember except how to clean the floor, how to do the dishes, how to eat our food quietly. As to the rest of all that extraneous stuff we carry around with us, we just let it go.

We worry, as we get older, about losing our memories. Some people do, that is. I don't. I find I'm remembering too much. For some people, a life review seems to be important for their spiritual development. Is this necessary, or is this just a way of shoring up the ego? A deep investigation of what has happened at some crucial point or other may be helpful to our actions in the present, but to go over and over and over it seems a great waste of time and energy. For some people, obsessing about what happened and holding on to painful memories goes on for as long as ten years or more. Let it go. We have this wonderful opportunity to practice in our precious tradition. Every activity is the practice of the Dharma. With a simple and direct mind we are engaged in this. And in doing this, we find the Buddha-light right here, in this very place. To understand this is really to experience zazen. And then, above all, remember that the foremost admonition of this practice, from generation to generation, from country to country, from culture to culture, is that we are doing this for the sake of all sentient beings. To have deep compassion for all beings, to extend This Mind, to radiate this Buddha-light over the whole universe: this is our enlightenment.

The ox pulls on the rope and almost breaks it. This ox-mind needs strong discipline, strong training. That is what we are doing here. We all have pain, we all become tired, but we stay with it. Every single moment we sit together is precious. We are helping one another see into our own true nature. It's not just our own thing, our own little pain, our own discipline. Our bodies, minds, and spirits are joined in this, and we do this for the sake of all sentient beings.

As our minds become clearer and more stable, the ox becomes quieter. In the last pictures, the stage of practice when our true Buddha-nature, our true self, has appeared, the ox has disappeared completely. There is nothing there. Everything has been forgotten.

28

The Most Intimate Connection

HUI-NENG HAD a difficult life, envied by some monks and priests and criticized by others, but he went straight ahead, practicing, teaching, working. Then it came time to die. His last words to his disciples were, "After my passing you must not lament or weep or wear mourning or receive condolences; you must strive only to know your own original mind and to see your own original nature."

Somebody came to me recently and said she was confused, because a famous teacher had told her to think about death, and she thought she should think about life. But of course they go together. Living, dying, living, dying. Life and death matters are Zen matters. Life is so precious, we should feel as if every single breath of it might be our last; we should make the most of it. Every single day, however ordinary, is extraordinary. Another person came and said she had read an essay that said life was mostly about middles; there were great highs and great lows, but mostly it was middles. She thought this made it sound awfully dull. Is this how we feel? Make the middles extraordinary middles! Every day is a good day if useless things do not clutter up the mind. Make the ordinary extraordinary.

We experience this every day during sesshin: everything becomes clearer, everything shines. We walk into the kitchen and the vegetables are leaping with light and energy, the peanut butter is glistening! Ordinary things are extraordinary because of what is going on in our minds. If we have a middling mind, we'll have middles. If we are awake and aware and practicing every single minute—not just on the cushion—everything is glowing and dynamic, not muddling middling.

So Hui-neng told his monks that after his passing they should not lament. Don't mourn, he said; don't waste energy on all this silly stuff; get on with it. Just find out about your own original nature. In Zen temples, when the master dies, all the disciples recite the sutras before the cremation, and then they give three wonderful loud cries, "Ai, ai, ai!" and that's it. Finished! Do not burst into tears or wear mourning or receive condolences, Hui-neng instructed. I hope you follow his instructions when I die, too. Have a great celebration, but no mourning.

Lao-tzu said, "The master came at the right time into the world; when his time was up, he left it again. He who submits when his work is done—in his life there is no room for sorrow."

If your mind is uncluttered, you cannot say a word in condolence. Silence is the deepest condolence. To see your own original Mind is the main point. Before your father and mother, what was your original face? Before the creation of the world, what were you? This is the fundamental koan. If you were not there, you would never be here. If you were there, before creation, what were you? This is not an individual matter. This does not belong to your egocentric consciousness at all. This is a universal wakefulness. You are here to know This Mind, to swallow up everything. Swallow the whole universe, and then you will know what Zen is. This Mind expands into the whole universe. It's not just a matter of your little tiny seat in it.

When sesshin is over, we feel a deep bond with one another. We have not spoken with one another, we have maintained this wonderful silence, yet we feel closely connected. One young woman came for just a couple of days, and she said to me at the beginning, "This is so strange to me. I come from a tradition where we talk a lot, express our feelings, share things, hug and touch; you don't do any of that. Can you explain why?"

"Sit for two days and see what happens," I told her. "I'm not going to explain why. You see how it feels to you. The only thing I can tell you is that some of us feel that this is the most intimate connection we can have with another human being: to sit together in deep silence." So after her two days, she came to my room upstairs and wept. "Yes," she said. "I see what you mean." And although she is leaving this part of the world, she said she feels deeply connected, and will support us in whatever way she can, and will return whenever she can. There was no need to make a big explanation to her; she experienced it, and felt as we all feel that we are much wider and deeper than anything we can say.

What gets in the way of understanding this? Some people come up to my little room and say they're stuck, they don't feel right, they can't understand it, they can't get it. What is there to get? Who is stuck? The ego, of course, wants to get something. You came here to get something: you want to get enlightenment, you want to change something in your life. But when the ego insists on getting, getting, it sticks itself up against everything: "*I* want, *I* must have, *I* need, this is *my* practice." Obstacles and contradictions are all rooted in ego. Some people are afraid to let go because then they may lose this little identity. "Who am I if I don't hang on to myself," they think. Of course you know you have a self, otherwise you wouldn't be here. If you didn't have some strong feeling of identity, you never would have come. You want to experience more in your life; you want to dig deeply into this mysterious, marvelous whatever-it-is, and not go around for the rest of your life thirsty and hungry.

Today is a wonderful, fresh day. With dynamic composure, go directly to what has to be done, cutting off all extraneous matters with no blinking, no hesitation. Just inquire, "Who is this noble person, this true person without rank? What is my original face before my parents were born?" Indeed, no words are necessary. "Who am I?" Even that is unnecessary. Don't cling to yesterday. You may have had some wonderful experience yesterday or you may have had some terrible experience; but there is just today, moment after moment. Each sitting is the only sitting, the very first sitting, the most extraordinary ordinary sitting.

29

The Last Word

THERE IS NOTHING that is not sacred; nothing that is not spiritual practice. Hakuin, that wonderful eighteenth-century Zen master who restored the vitality of Zen in Japan, warned against the belief that Zen requires the forceful rejection of all worldly concerns. True Zen practice is carried on in the midst of activity. When we are cooking, we are in deep cooking samadhi. When we are cleaning, we are in deep cleaning samadhi. This condition, samadhi, is not a vacancy, a stupor, a spaced-out state of mind. It is a deeply awake, alert, vividly present condition—and of course, it may be blissful. We may be so vividly awake we can hear the ash from the incense fall.

Each of the activities we are engaged in, when given our full attention, without any feeling of resentment or comparison, is an opportunity to experience something, to open our eyes more clearly. When we let go of our egocentric hold on things, we find that something wonderful is there, something that has always been there; we have never been without it.

Just throw everything away, including anything I may say, including any good condition that may arise. Just go on. No condition is permanent. Don't hold on to anything. Become the smoke from the incense. Drop off the habit of interfering with what happens and you will sense your mind becoming healthier, stronger. Accepting your discomforts or frustrations rather than repressing or avoiding them, allowing changes in yourself, you will experience your true self.

Chanting the Three Refuges, as we do each day, we feel something just from the beautiful sounds themselves. Taking refuge in the Buddha, the Dharma, and the Sangha is a means of dissolving the ego, throwing away our selfishness, offering ourselves. Taking refuge, we stand in the knowledge that our true nature is clear-minded, warm-hearted. We are following the endless path of the bodhisattva, the path of practice, and of action.

Our balancing of wisdom and compassion is always changing, growing, maturing, being directed into the various circumstances of our lives. When do we do enough, and when do we do too much? And what do we ask of people? This is a very subtle matter.

We must be aware that we do not help others when we do too much for them. And we do not help ourselves when we ask too much from others. Each of us is here to stand on our own two feet. We are supported by the wonderful practice of everyone around us, but we must do our own practice, by ourselves. We must discover it for ourselves. We cannot say to someone else, "Please help me." Help yourself! It's all right there in front of you—help yourself. Do not impose on other people's kindness, begging for help. This is exceedingly important.

There was a Zen master named Seppo, who lived in China at a time when there was severe persecution of Buddhism. One day two monks, who no doubt had been to see many other masters, came to his little hermitage. They expected something from Seppo, who was at the prime of his maturity. They came to the gate. Seppo pushed open the gate joyfully, seeing two self-assured young gentlemen walking along the road, and thinking, ah, there will be some wonderful confrontation; what will come of it? He opened the gate, and said, "What is this?" What did they do? They just came back with the same words: "What is this?" Did they just imitate him, or had they really understood something? He turned away and walked back to his cottage.

What is this? If you went to Seppo and he asked you, "What is this?" how would you respond? These koans, these questions are for us. What is this? How do you express it? Not by sitting down and thinking about it, but by continuing to practice, until suddenly, like a flower ready to bloom, vroom! Here it is! This is your Zen expression. Got it? Another three years, ten years, thirty years, however many years, to come to your own expression, as with all great artists. Zen is an art. There are no imitations, there's no using a phrase from a book. What is your own phrase? What is your own life expression?

At first these two monks may have thought they had defeated Seppo by quickly responding with his own phrase, but later they thought about it, and they wondered. They decided to go see Ganto, who was a friend of Seppo and might be able to explain it to them. Hearing their story, Ganto said, "If Seppo had been given the last word, then you would never have been able to feel that you had defeated him."

The monks spent the summer with Ganto, and continued to ponder their encounter with Seppo. At the end of the summer, the monks met with Ganto again, who told them, "Seppo and I had our eyes opened in the same way." He was saying, "We both are enlightened people." And then he told them, "But we are dying in different ways." This dying didn't mean dying as in ending life, but dying as in giving it all away, giving everything away: teaching. "What is this?" was Seppo's way of teaching. Ganto's way was "the last word." Rinzai's way was "kwatz!" Gutei's way was "one finger." These are all different ways of giving it away.

What is this last word? Ganto said, "If you want to know the last word, I'll tell you: *This.*" There is no last word. There is no end to it. Somebody told me, "I have finished my Zen training.

I have answered all 1,700 koans." I replied, "Well, you've just begun." Nobody finishes this training. There is no last word. *This* is a present-tensed word, going on forever. What is your own experience of This?

Glossary

NOTE: Since Maurine Stuart's Zen teachers were Japanese, she tended to use Japanese names and terminology (with a few exceptions, like Avalokitesvara, Bodhidharma, Hui-neng, Vimilakirti, and the more familiar Sanskrit terms). I have followed her usage, and have provided the Chinese or Sanskrit equivalents in each case.

AMIDA, Japanese (Sanskrit: Amitabha): The Buddha of boundless light, ruler of what is variously called the Western Paradise, Sukhavati, the Pure Land. Amida is venerated in Pure Land Buddhism through the repetition of the mantra "Namu Amida Butsu," meaning "to become one with Amida Buddha" or "homage to Amida Buddha." *See* Jodo Shinshu.

AVALOKITESVARA, Skt. (J.: Kannon or Kanzeon): The bodhisattva who sees the suffering of all beings, who hears all cries. Avalokitesvara is the embodiment of compassion, just as Manjusri is the embodiment of wisdom. Iconographically, Avalokitesvara is often depicted with a thousand arms, with an eye in the palm of each hand, and eleven faces. *See* bodhisattva.

BASHASHITA, J. (Skt.: Vashashita): The twenty-sixth lineage-holder after Shakyamuni Buddha; said to have been born holding a jewel given to him in his former life by a Buddhist master. *See* Funyomitta.

BODHI, Skt.: Perfect wisdom; enlightenment; awakening to one's own Buddha-nature.

BODHIDHARMA, Skt. (J.: Bodaidaruma or Daruma): The twenty-eighth master after Shakyamuni in the Indian lineage, who traveled from India to China in 520 C.E. and is considered the first ancestral teacher of Zen. He emphasized the direct experience of seeing into one's true nature rather than relying on scriptures or the formulations of others.

BODHISATTVA, Skt. (J.: bosatsu or bosa): An enlightened being who understands realization not as a personal goal, not as an end in itself, but as a means to liberate all beings from suffering, and who dedicates her or himself to manifesting compassion and wisdom in daily life.

BOMPU, J.: Ordinary, or deluded, consciousness; an egocentric view of the world.

BUDDHA, Skt. and Pali (J.: Butsu or Bu): Literally, "enlightened one." The historical Buddha is Shakyamuni Buddha (563–483 B.C.E.). The son of a prince of the Shakya clan, his personal name was Siddhartha Gautama. Through his awakening he realized that fundamentally all beings are buddhas, and that there is a path of liberation that can be taught, received, and followed. The term is also used to refer to buddhas who preceded Shakyamuni, like his teacher, Dipankara, and to the buddha who will renew the Dharma in the future age, Maitreya. Other buddhas, like Amitabha and Vairocana, are held to be teachers of the bodhisattvas; each is the mystical personification of a Pure Land.

BUDDHA-DHARMA, Skt.: Buddha-teaching, or fundamental law, which cannot be understood conceptually but must be grasped intuitively through the experience of enlightenment. The manifestation of true nature in all phenomena. *See* Dharma.

CHU KOKUSHI, J. (Chin.: Chung-kuo-shih): The T'ang dynasty Zen master Nanyo Echu (Chin.: Nan-yang Hui-chung) who, after long years of training with the Sixth Patriarch, Hui-neng, became his Dharma successor and then spent forty years in seclusion in order to deepen his understanding. At the age of eighty-five, he reluctantly accepted the position of master to the Emperor Su-tsung and to the succeeding Emperor Tai-tsung, thus receiving the honorary title "Teacher of the Country" (J.: Kokushi; Chin.: kuo-shih).

DAIO KOKUSHI: Nampo Shomyo, a Japanese Rinzai Zen master who lived from 1235–1309, who was given the honorary title "Great

Teacher of the Country" (J.: Daio Kokushi). He traveled to China in 1259 and received transmission from Kido Chigu (Chin.: Hsu-t'ang Chih-yu) before returning to Japan. Later masters in this lineage were the formidable Ikkyu Sojun and Hakuin Ekaku. "Kokushi" means National Teacher.

DHARMA, Skt.: A key term in Buddhism with many meanings, the first of which is phenomenon. Physical phenomena and mental constructs are subject to the law of causation; another meaning of Dharma is law, or truth. Still another meaning is the teachings of the Buddha, whose realization penetrated into the fundamental truth of the universe.

DHYANA, Skt.: Meditation, intensive absorption of mind; the fifth of the six paramitas. Since the time of Hui-neng, dhyana and prajna, the sixth paramita, have been seen as inseparable in Zen practice. In China, dhyana became Ch'an, and was transliterated to the term Zen in Japan. *See* paramita; prajna.

DOGEN: Eihei Dogen Kigen (1200–53) trained for nine years under the Rinzai master Myoan Eisai before traveling to China, where he studied with and became the Dharma heir of Tendo Nyojo (Chin.: T'ien-t'ung Ju-ching). He brought the teachings of the Soto (Chin.: Ts'ao-tung-tsung) school of Zen from China back to Japan, where he established Eihei-ji, which became the principal Soto training monastery. Dogen wrote many important essays on Zen, the best-known collection of which is the *Shobogenzo* (Treasury of the True Dharma Eye). In his teachings he criticized what he saw as signs of degeneration and formulaic practices among Rinzai adherents; he stressed the importance of zazen as the sole route to enlightenment—and at the same time, warned against striving for enlightenment. *See* Soto.

DOKUSAN, J.: Private, formal encounters between teacher and student, particularly important in Rinzai Zen practice; usually held two or three times a day during sesshin.

EKA, J. (Chin.: Hui-k'o): The Dharma successor of Bodhidharma and second ancestral teacher of Zen in China. His desperate desire for genuine insight is recorded in Case 41 of the *Gateless Gate* (see "Peace of Mind" p. 72 in this volume).

ENGO, J. (Chin.: Yuan-wu K'o-ch'in): Engo Kokugon (1063–1135), the Dharma successor of Goso Hoen (Chin.: Wu-tsu Fa-yen), was the editor of the *Blue Cliff Record,* to which he contributed commentaries, introductions, and notes. His Dharma successors included Daie

Soko (Chin.: Ta-hui Tsung-kao), who played a major role in the evolution of koan practice. Hakuin Ekaku, who revitalized Rinzai Zen in Japan, was also in this lineage.

FOUR GREAT Vows: Recited daily by Zen practitioners, they are: "However innumerable all beings are, I vow to save them all. However inexhaustible delusions are, I vow to extinguish them all. However immeasurable Dharma teachings are, I vow to master them all. However endless the Buddha's way is, I vow to follow it."

FUNYOMITTA, J. (Skt.: Punyamitra): A prince whose grandfather had venerated the Buddhist teacher Bashashita (Skt.: Vashashita), the twenty-sixth spiritual descendant from Shakyamuni. After his grandfather's death, Funyomitta's father, who was a Hindu, became king, and challenged Bashashita. When Funyomitta admonished his father for this, he was imprisoned. Later, after a significant encounter with Bashashita, the king had an about-face and pardoned his son, who then became a monk and, eventually, Bashashita's successor.

GANTO, J. (Chin.: Yen-t'ou Chuan-huo): Ganto Zenkatsu (828–87), a Dharma successor of Zuigan Shigen (Chin.: Te-shan Hsuan-chien), appears in Case 13 of the *Gateless Gate* and in cases 51 and 66 of the *Blue Cliff Record.*

GASSHO, J.: The gesture of reverence, of greeting, of gratitude, and of expressing oneness with all beings, made by putting the palms of the hands together.

GOSO, J. (Chin.: Wu-tsu Fa-yen): Goso Hoen (ca. 1024–1104), a Dharma successor of Hakuun Shutan (Chin.: Pai-yun Shou-tuan), appears in cases 35, 36, 38, and 45 of the *Gateless Gate.*

GUTEI, J. (Chin.: Chu-chih): Very little is known about this Zen master, who lived in China in or around the ninth century; he appears in the well-known Case 3 of the *Gateless Gate.*

HAN, J.: Literally, "board," the wooden instrument that typically hangs just outside the zendo (meditation hall), and is struck at dawn and dusk—when the lines in the palm of one's hand can no longer be seen—and before retiring. The back of the han often bears an inscription that reads, "Listen, followers of the Way! Be diligent with your practice. Time flies like an arrow. It doesn't wait for you!"

HARA, J.: Also known as *kikai tanden,* it refers both to the physical center of the body and to the locus of spiritual power in the lower abdomen. Regulating the breath so that it is focused in the hara results in the accumulation of samadhi energy essential to zazen, and fosters the experiential understanding that mind and body are one.

HOGEN, J. (Chin.: Fa-yen Wen-i): Hogen Bun'eki (885–958) had sixty-three Dharma successors, and his school flourished for three generations, spreading throughout China and into Korea. He is encountered in Case 26 of the *Gateless Gate* and Case 7 of the *Blue Cliff Record.*

HUI-NENG, Chin. (J.: Eno): Often referred to as the Sixth Patriarch (638–713). One of the most influential figures in Zen history, Hui-neng brought a refreshing directness and originality to Zen Buddhism; his teachings were accessible to those who, like himself, were not learned scholars. Many legends grew up around him, and found their way into the putatively autobiographical section of the *Platform Sutra,* a compilation of his teachings by his disciples. According to this section, his father died when he was three; he worked as a woodcutter, and was illiterate; his spiritual journey began when he happened to hear the passage from the *Diamond Sutra,* "Depending on nothing, realize your own mind"; he trained with Hung-jen, who told his disciples one day that whoever could write a poem conveying true understanding would succeed him to become the Sixth Patriarch. Hui-neng's verse was selected over that of the head monk, Shen-hsiu. The head monk's verse stressed "polishing the mirror" of the mind so that no dust obscured its clarity; in his verse, Hui-neng declared, "Buddha-nature is always clean and pure; Where is there room for dust?"

HYAKUJO, J. (Chin.: Pai-chang Huai-hai): Hyakujo Ekai (720–814) was the Dharma heir of Baso Doitsu (Chin.: Ma-tsu Tao-i). He founded the Zen monastic tradition in China, laying down rules of conduct and emphasizing a balance between zazen and physical labor. It was he who said, "A day of not working is a day of not eating." He is also regarded as the originator of the tea ceremony. His talks were compiled by his disciples as *Sayings and Doings of Pai-Chang* (translated into English by Thomas Cleary). He appears in cases 2 and 40 of the *Gateless Gate,* and in cases 26, 53, 70, 71, 72, and 73 of the *Blue Cliff Record.* His Dharma heirs included Isan Reiyu (Chin.: Kuei-shan Ling-yu) and Obaku Kiun (Chin.: Huang-po Hsi-yun).

INKA, J.: *Inka shomei,* literally "seal of acknowledgment" by a Zen master that a student has reached profound maturity in his or her training, which includes passing the requisite number of koans, manifesting genuine insight, and demonstrating the ability to teach others. With this acknowledgment of transmission from mind to mind, the student is proclaimed the master's Dharma heir, and may be addressed as roshi. In the Rinzai tradition the conferring of inka is rare, and of great consequence.

ISAN, J. (Chin.: Kuei-shan Ling-yu): Isan Reiyu (771–853) was a successor of Hyakujo Ekai, with whom he spent twenty years as tenzo (the senior disciple in charge of the kitchen). He had some fifteen hundred students, produced forty-three Dharma heirs, and his sayings and teachings were recorded in a book. Isan appears in Case 40 of the *Gateless Gate* and in cases 4, 24, and 70 of the *Blue Cliff Record*.

JIKIJITSU, J.: The leader and timekeeper of the zendo in Rinzai Zen, responsible for maintaining a strong and alert atmosphere. Literally, "jiki" means straight, and "jitsu" means day, implying one who sits straight through the entire day.

JI and RI, J.: "Thing-principle"; the particular event and the universal truth; form and formlessness; the relative and the absolute. Ji refers to learned behavior, or technique; ri is intuitive understanding, inner freedom.

JIZO, J. (Skt.: Kshitigarbha): A bodhisattva venerated as the protector of children, travelers, and vulnerable people in general. Also, a ninth-century Chinese master (Chin.: Ti-ts'ang) known for his mondo with his principal student Hogen Bun'eki (Chin.: Fa-yen wen-i).

JODO SHINSHU, J.: "True School of the Pure Land," founded by Shinran (1173–1262); also known as Shin Buddhism, and the most popular form of Buddhism in Japan. As in the Jodo Shu ("School of the Pure Land"), followers place absolute trust in Amida Buddha (Skt.: Amitabha). The teaching emphasizes that the sincere and repetitive recitation of the formula "Namu Amida Butsu" will result in rebirth as a buddha in the Pure Land. In the Jodo Shinshu, this recitation is done as an expression of gratitude on the part of the believer. For the Jodo Shu adherent, the recitation itself deepens the trust in Amida, in "other power." *See* Amida.

JOSHU, J. (Chin.: Chao-chou Ts'ung-shen): Joshu Jushin (778–897) experienced profound enlightenment at the age of eighteen. He then trained for forty more years under Nansen Fugan (Chin.: Nanch'uan P'u-yuan), and after Nansen's death he made pilgrimages to deepen his realization further. He did not begin teaching until the age of eighty, when he settled in a small monastery in the town of Chao-chou. He is best known through the koan in which he answered a monk's question, "Does a dog have Buddha-nature or not?" with the succinct reply, "Mu!" (Case 1 of the *Gateless Gate*). He also appears in cases 7, 11, 14, 19, 31, and 37 of that collection, and in cases 2, 9, 30, 41, 45, 52, 57, 58, 59, 64, 80, and 96 of the *Blue Cliff Record*. See Mu.

JUKAI, J.: The ceremony in which a lay practitioner receives the Buddhist precepts, ethical guidelines governing behavior, and dedicates her or himself to the path. *See* precepts.

KANNON: *See* Avalokitesvara.

KARUNA, Skt. and Pali: Compassion, loving sympathy that flows without discrimination toward all beings. In tandem with prajna (wisdom), karuna is the chief attribute of all buddhas and bodhisattvas; especially associated with Avalokitesvara.

KEISAKU, J.: Also kyosaku. Literally, "wake-up stick," a long, flat, wooden stick carried with respectful attentiveness by a senior student or monk during zazen periods. Those who request it are struck on each shoulder or on the back. Providing relief from muscle tension and fatigue, as well as intensifying the atmosphere, the keisaku is used only to encourage a student's practice, never to punish.

KENSHO, J.: Also satori. An essential element in Rinzai Zen, usually translated as realization, awakening, or enlightenment. Kensho refers to the liberating experience of breaking through the ego-driven, self-preoccupied view of reality to the clear understanding of things just as they are. *Ken* means "seeing into"; *sho* means "one's own nature."

KESA, J. (transliteration of Skt.: *kashaya*): A ceremonial robe used by fully ordained practitioners. Draped over the left shoulder, the kesa is symbolic of the patchwork garment worn by monks in India during Shakyamuni Buddha's time. The abbreviated version used during zazen and other nonceremonial activities is the *rakusu,* worn over the chest.

KESSEI, J.: Three-month training period in a Zen monastery, also called *ango.*

KINHIN, J.: Walking meditation done between periods of zazen; a transition between motionless practice and the practice of daily life.

KOAN, J.: Literally, "public case"; taken from the Chinese *kung-an*. A key element of Rinzai Zen practice and sometimes used in the Soto school as well, a koan is constructed from a recorded encounter between a master and a student, a sutra, or teaching, and is used to spur the practitioner toward breaking free of habitual responses and intellectual concepts. Koans cannot be solved by logical analysis; they require full-bore intuitive concentration. Intensive koan practice, particularly during sesshin, can result in self-realization. *See* kensho.

KOSEN: Kosen Soon (1816–92), known by his family name of Kosen Imakita, was an influential Zen master of the Meiji era whose breadth of knowledge ranged from the Chinese classics to European philosophy. He was the author of *A Wave on the Zen Sea,* a highly regarded text integrating Buddhism and Confucianism, and served as abbot of Eiko-ji in Iwakuni from 1858 to 1875, and then of Engaku-ji from 1875 to 1892. His Dharma heir was Kogaku Soen Shaku, who brought Zen to America.

KYOSEI, J. (Chin.: Ching-ch'ing Tao-fu): Kyosei Dofu (863/68–937) was the Dharma heir of Seppo Gison (Chin.: Hsueh-feng I'ts'un), and appears in cases 6, 23, and 46 of the *Blue Cliff Record.*

KYOZAN, J. (Chin.: Yang-shan Hui-chi): Kyozan Ejaku (807–883) was such an inspiring Zen master that he was called Little Shakyamuni. As a youth, he studied with the great masters Baso Doitsu (Chin.: Ma-tsu Tao-i) and Hyakujo Ekai (Chin.: Pai-chang Huai-hai), and was the Dharma successor of Isan Reiyu (Chin.: Kuei-shan Lingyu), under whom he realized profound enlightenment. He appears in Case 25 of the *Gateless Gate* and cases 34 and 68 of the *Blue Cliff Record.*

MAHAYANA, Skt.: Literally, "Great Vehicle," referring to its emphasis on attaining liberation for the sake of all beings, thus broadening the scope of earlier Buddhism's emphasis on individual realization. Zen is one of the schools based in the Mahayana branch of Buddhism. The Mahayana view is that one's true nature is from the beginning liberated; the realization and actualization of this are embodied in the way of the bodhisattva. *See* Theravada.

MANJUSRI, Skt. (J.: Monju): Literally, "the noble and gentle one." The bodhisattva of wisdom, he is usually depicted with an ignorance-dispelling sword in his right hand and a volume of the *Prajnaparamita* literature in his left.

MAYOKU, J. (Chin.: Ma-ku Pao-che): Mayoku Hotetsu, a T'ang dynasty Zen master, was the Dharma successor of Baso Doitsu (Chin.: Ma-tsu Tao-i), and appears in Case 31 of the *Blue Cliff Record.*

MONDO, J.: A Zen dialogue in which a question about fundamental reality is answered in a way that expresses that reality, cutting through conceptualization and allowing the questioner to realize it directly.

MU, J. (Chin.: wu): The syllable Zen students know best, from Case 1 of the *Gateless Gate:* A monk asked Joshu (Chin.: Chao-chou), "Does a dog have Buddha-nature or not?" Joshu answered, *"Mu!"* Literally, Mu means no, none, or nothing; logically, of course, such an answer goes against what the monk has been taught: that all beings have Buddha-nature. In Zen practice, Mu is used to delve deeply into the profundity of this "no."

MU-SHIN, J.: Literally, "no-mind"; the natural, at-rest condition in which the mind is emptied of the commentaries, plans, fantasies, judgments, and memories that usually hold forth.

MUMON, J. (Chin.: Wu-men Hui-k'ai): Mumon Ekai (1183–1260) compiled the *Gateless Gate* (J.: *Mumonkan;* Chin.: *Wu-men-kuan*), a collection of forty-eight koans for which he wrote the accompanying commentaries and verses. His own six-year struggle with Mu resulted in a profound awakening, and later, when he composed the *Gateless Gate,* he made "Joshu's 'Mu'" the first case in that collection. His disciple and Dharma successor Shinchi Kakushin brought a copy of the *Gateless Gate,* written in Mumon's own hand, back to Japan with him in 1254.

MYOSHO, J. (Chin.: Ming-chao Te-chien): Myosho Tokken was a well-known teacher in China around the tenth century. A Dharma successor of Rakan Dokan (Chin.: Lo-han Tao-hsien), he was also called the One-eyed Dragon, having lost his left eye. He is encountered in Case 48 of the *Blue Cliff Record.*

NANSEN, J. (Chin.: Nan-ch'uan P'u-yuan) (748–835), Dharma heir of Baso Doitsu (Chin.: Ma-tsu Tao-i), was renowned for his dynamic and paradoxical way of expressing his understanding. Among his seventeen Dharma successors was the mighty Joshu Jushin (Chin.: Chao-chou Ts'ung-shen).

NEN, J.: Intensive mind; consciousness vibrantly at one with the present moment.

NIRVANA, Skt.: Literally, extinction. In Mahayana Buddhism, often regarded as extinction of the dualistic views (including birth and death) that cause suffering. A condition beyond conceptualization in which the identity of the relative and the absolute is experienced. Parinirvana, complete extinction, is usually used to refer to Shakyamuni Buddha's passing away.

NIWAZUME, J.: The strenuous trial period to which, traditionally, one is subjected before being admitted to a monastery. It is spent kneeling in a prescribed posture for two or three days, and is meant to test one's sincerity, commitment, and powers of endurance.

OBAKU, J. (Chin.: Huang-po Hsi-yun): Obaku Kiun, who died in 850, was a Dharma heir of Hyakujo Ekai (Chin.: Pai-chang Huai-hai), and among his own thirteen successors was Rinzai Gigen (Chin.: Lin-chi I-hsuan). His recorded talks and dialogues were compiled in *The Zen Teaching of Huang Po: On the Transmission of Mind,* one of the most influential Zen texts (translated into English by John Blofeld). Obaku appears in Case 2 of the *Gateless Gate* and Case 11 of the *Blue Cliff Record.*

PARAMITA, Skt.: Literally, "having reached the other shore." The six paramitas are the perfections, or virtues, characteristic of a bodhisattva: *dana* (generosity), *sila* (morality or precepts), *ksanti* (patience or tolerance), *virya* (diligence), *dhyana* (meditation), and *prajna* (wisdom). By means of their practice, the other shore is realized to be none other than this shore, the here and now.

PRAJNA, Skt.: Wisdom, or intuitive mind. Prajna is the sixth paramita. It was one of Hui-neng's most important (and revolutionary) teachings that prajna is not some separate condition to be attained as a result of dhyana, but is the simultaneous functioning of dhyana. *See* dhyana.

PRECEPTS: Ethical guidelines governing the behavior of Buddhist monks, nuns, and lay practitioners. In jukai, the ceremony of receiving the precepts, one vows to observe the Three Fundamental Precepts: to refrain from all evil, to practice all that is good, and to keep one's heart and mind pure. After taking the Three Refuges (in the Buddha, the Dharma, and the Sangha), one vows to uphold the Ten Precepts, which are: to be reverential toward all life; to respect others' property; to free oneself from lust; to honor honesty; to abstain from intoxicants; to avoid gossip; to refrain from praising oneself and judging others; to allow gratitude to replace envy and jealousy; to avoid giving way to anger; and to esteem the Three Treasures, Buddha, Dharma, and Sangha.

RAKUSU, J.: A rectangular, pieced-together vestment that hangs on the chest from a strap around the neck. Symbolic of the patched robes worn by Shakyamuni Buddha and his disciples, and received when taking the precepts, the rakusu is the abbreviated form of the kesa (which is worn only by monks and nuns). *See* kesa.

RI: *See* JI and RI.

RINZAI, J. (Chin.: Lin-chi I-hsuan): Rinzai Gigen, who died in 866 or 867, founded what became the most influential Buddhist sect of T'ang-dynasty China, the Rinzai School. Rinzai and Soto Zen are the two major schools of Zen in Japan and the West. Rinzai was known for his abrupt and dynamic methods of awakening students, which included shouts ("Kwatz!") and unexpected blows. His training style was the culmination of Zen's development from Hui-neng (J.: Eno) through Obaku (Chin.: Huang-po), from whom he received Dharma transmission. Rinzai had twenty-one successors, and appears in cases 20 and 32 of the *Blue Cliff Record*. The compilation of his teachings in the *Rinzai Roku* is still a vital text for Zen students.

RINZAI ROKU, J.: The recorded sayings of Rinzai (Chin.: Lin-chi I-hsuan), translated into English by Ruth F. Sasaki as *The Record of Lin-chi* (Kyoto: Institute for Zen Studies, 1975) and by Burton Watson as *The Zen Teachings of Master Lin-chi* (Boston: Shambhala, 1993).

ROHATSU, J.: The eighth day of the twelfth month, when the enlightenment of Shakyamuni Buddha is commemorated. According to tradition, he had been doing deep meditation under the bodhi tree when he saw the morning star and had a profound awakening. Rohatsu sesshin, held in most Zen monasteries and centers from the evening of November 30 through the morning of December 8, is the most rigorous and demanding retreat of the year.

ROSHI, J.: Literally, venerable or old master. In the Rinzai tradition it is reserved for one who has undergone long years of strenuous training, has manifested deep insight, maturity, and leadership, and has received inka, the seal of Dharma transmission.

SAMADHI, Skt.: One-pointed concentration; the state of mind during deep zazen that is unimpeded and undifferentiating. Phenomena are experienced just as they are, with no interference.

SAMANTABHADRA, Skt. (J.: Fugen): Usually depicted in tandem with Manjusri, the bodhisattva of wisdom, Samantabhadra exemplifies beneficence, and is often shown riding a white, six-tusked elephant, symbolic of overcoming attachment to the six senses and other obstacles.

SANGHA, Skt.: One of the three treasures of Buddhism, along with Buddha and Dharma. Historically, Sangha refers to the assembly that gathered around Shakyamuni Buddha; the broader reference is to a community of Buddhist practitioners, lay and ordained.

SATORI: *See* kensho.

SEIHO, J. (Chin.: Ch'ing Lin): Little is known of Seiho except that he was the teacher of a monk who then spent three years with Hogen without going to see him for dokusan. See the Commentary to Case 7 of the *Blue Cliff Record,* translated by Thomas Cleary and J. C. Cleary (Boston: Shambhala, 1992).

SEPPO, J. (Chin.: Hsueh-feng I'ts'un): Seppo Gison (822–908) was the Dharma heir of Tokusan Senkan (Chin.: Te-shan Hsuan-chien). Among his fifty-six Dharma successors was Ummon Bun'en (Chin.: Yun-men Wen-yen). Seppo first expressed his desire to become a monk at the age of nine, but at his parents' request, postponed his ordination—although he lived at a monastery from twelve on. After studying with several well-known teachers, he went to live on Hsueh-feng (Snowy Peak); within ten years some fifteen hundred disciples had gathered there. In 882 he was given the title "Truly Enlightened Great Teacher" by the Emperor I Tsung. Seppo appears in Case 13 of the *Gateless Gate* and in cases 5, 22, 49, 51 and 66 of the *Blue Cliff Record.*

SESSHIN, J.: Literally, to collect or join *(setsu)* the heart-mind *(shin),* sesshin is a period of three, five, or seven days during which students single-mindedly engage in zazen (meditation). Strict silence is maintained throughout. In Rinzai communities, a daily teisho or Dharma talk is given by the teacher or a senior student, and dokusan is conducted two or three times a day.

SHAKU, SOYEN: A Dharma heir of Kosen Imakita, Kogaku Soyen Shaku (1859–1919) took a great interest in Western culture and philosophy. He was the first Zen master to visit America from Japan. He addressed the World Parliament of Religions in Chicago in 1893, and then in 1905 made a second visit, one even more important to the development of Zen practice in the West. He stayed for nearly a year at the home of Mrs. Alexander Russell in San Francisco, giving frequent talks on Buddhism at the request of his hostess, who has been called "the gate-opener of Zen in America," and addressing audiences on both coasts, before making a European tour. His students, D. T. Suzuki and Nyogen Senzaki, carried on his transmission of Zen to the West.

SHAKYAMUNI, Skt.: The name by which Siddhartha Gautama came to be known (literally, "Sage of the Shakyas"). *See* Buddha.

SHIDO: The founder of Tokei-ji, a convent on a hill facing Engaku-ji.

Shido was the consort or wife of the warrior-regent Hojo Toki-
mune, who supported and studied with several important Chinese
Zen masters in Japan, and who established Engaku-ji. After his
death in 1284, she took nun's vows and withdrew to Tokei-ji, which
became a refuge for women who had been divorced or ill-treated
by their husbands.

SHUZAN, J. (Chin.: Shou-shan Sheng-nien): Shuzan Shonen (926–993),
a Zen master in the Rinzai lineage who was the Dharma successor
of Fuketsu Ensho (Chin.: Feng-hsueh Yen-chao), is seen in Case 43
of the *Gateless Gate*.

SILA: *See* precepts.

SOSAN, J. (Chin.: Seng-ts'an): Third ancestral teacher in the Chinese
lineage after Bodhidharma and Eka (Chin.: Hui-k'o), Sosan Ganchi
(ca. 606) is known for his lengthy poem *On Believing in Mind* (J.:
Shinjinmei: Chin.: *Hsin-hsin-ming*), which conveys the basic princi-
ples of Zen. It begins with the well-known statement, "The great
Way is not difficult; it just refuses to make preferences," which is
referred to in many subsequent teachings, such as Case 2 of the *Blue
Cliff Record*.

SOTO, J.: One of the five schools of Zen that developed in China during
the T'ang dynasty. The Soto and Rinzai Schools are the dominant
forms of Zen in modern-day Japan and the West. The Soto tradition
was established by Tozan Ryokai (Chin.: Tung-shan Liang-chieh)
and his student Sozan Honjaku (Chin.: Ts'ao-shan Pen-chi); it was
brought to Japan by Dogen Kigen. In the Soto School, *shikantaza,*
just sitting, is the principal way of practice; the term "silent illumination" is also used.

SUNYATA, Skt. (J.: ku). Literally, "emptiness," or "voidness," but not in
a dualistic or nihilistic sense. To experience sunyata is to realize that
all composite things are fundamentally devoid of any fixed condition or substance; hence, to experience them as they are, with no
conceptual or preferential shadings. Sunyata is the key teaching in
the *Prajnaparamita Sutras,* the best known of which are the *Diamond
Sutra* and the *Heart Sutra*.

SUTRA, Skt.: Literally, the thread upon which the jewels of Shakyamuni Buddha's discourses were strung. There are said to be more
than ten thousand of these texts. Many were translated from the
original Pali and Sanskrit into Chinese and Tibetan; relatively few
have been translated into English. Each begins with the phrase

"Thus have I heard," the purported narrator being Shakyamuni Buddha's student Ananda, although sutras continued to be written centuries after the Buddha's death.

SUZUKI ROSHI: Shunryu Suzuki (1905–71) was one of the pioneers of Zen in America. A teacher of the Soto school, he came to America in 1958 for what he had intended to be a short visit, but was so impressed by the receptivity and seriousness of Americans interested in Zen that he decided to stay. He founded the Zen Center of San Francisco and the first Soto Zen monastery outside Asia, Zen Mountain Center at Tassajara, California. His recorded talks, edited by Trudy Dixon, were published as *Zen Mind, Beginner's Mind* (New York: Weatherhill) in 1970, and the book has become a classic text.

TATHAGATA, Skt. and Pali: *Tathata* means thusness, things as they are, or suchness. Tathagata may be translated "thus come, thus gone," referring to one who has attained buddhahood. In the sutras, Tathagata is a term used by Shakyamuni Buddha to refer to himself or to other buddhas.

TEISHO, J.: A Zen master's vivid, nonconceptual presentation of the Dharma, usually based on a traditional koan from such compilations as the *Gateless Gate*, the *Blue Cliff Record*, or the *Book of Equanimity*.

TENRYU, J. (Chin.: Hang-chou T'ien-lung): Koshu Tenryu was a Dharma successor of Daibai Hojo (Chin.: Ta-mei Fa-ch'ang); his student was Gutei (Chin.: Chuchih). Their encounter is described in Case 3 of the *Gateless Gate*.

TENZO, J.: The person in charge of the kitchen at a monastery. This crucial office is held by one who is deemed mature in his or her practice, since being tenzo is not merely a matter of preparing tasty and nutritious food, but of treating each ingredient with reverence, wasting neither time nor materials.

THERAVADA, Skt.: Literally, "Teaching of the Elders"; followers observe the strict rules set forth in the Vinaya-pitaka, the third part of the Tripitaka (the canon of Buddhist scriptures), in which every aspect of daily life and ceremonial life is precisely detailed. In so doing, it is believed, personal liberation can be obtained. *See* Mahayana.

THICH NHAT HANH: A Vietnamese Zen teacher who is active in the engaged Buddhism movement. He was nominated for the Nobel Peace Prize in 1967 by Martin Luther King, Jr., and headed the

Vietnamese Buddhist Peace Delegation during the Paris Peace Accords. A prolific author, he resides for much of the year at Plum Village, the Buddhist community he established in southwestern France.

TOKEI-JI: *See* Shido.

TOZAN, J. (Chin.: Tung-shan Liang-chieh): Tozan Ryokai (807–69) studied with many well-known teachers, including Nansen Fugan (Chin.: Nan-ch'uan P'u-yuan), Isan Reiyu (Chin.: Kuei-shan Ling-yu), and Ungan Donjo (Chin.: Yun-yen T'an-sheng). His own students were numerous; among his twenty-six Dharma heirs were Sozan Honjaku (Chin.: Ts'ao-shan Pen-chi), with whom he founded the Soto school, and Ungo Doyo (Chin.: Yun-chu Tao-ying). Tozan is also renowned in the Rinzai School for his formulation of "the five ranks of enlightenment" (see *Zen Dust*, by Isshu Miura and Ruth Fuller Sasaki). Clear insight into the five ranks is considered the culmination of koan training in Rinzai Zen. Tozan is encountered in Case 43 of the *Blue Cliff Record*.

UMMON, J. (Chin.: Yun-men Wen-yen): Ummon Bun'en (864–949) was the Dharma heir of Seppo Gison (Chin.: Hsueh-feng I'ts'un), and had more than sixty successors himself. Founder of the Ummon School, he used words in a vivid and dynamic way; no other master's sayings are encountered as frequently as his, in the *Gateless Gate* (cases 15, 16, 21, 39, and 48) and particularly in the *Blue Cliff Record* (cases 6, 8, 14, 15, 22, 27, 34, 39, 47, 50, 54, 60, 62, 77, 83, 86, 87, and 88). Many of his responses (often to questions he himself posed) are renowned as "one-word barriers."

UNGAN, J. (Chin.: Yun-yen T'an-sheng: Ungan Donjo (781–841) left home when still quite young and began his training under Hyakujo Ekai (Chin.: Pai-chang Huai-hai). After Hyakujo's death, Ungan became the student (and eventual Dharma heir) of Yakusan Igen (Chin.: Yao-shan Wei-yen). He is met in cases 70, 72, and 89 of the *Blue Cliff Record*.

VIMILAKIRTI, Skt. (J.: Yuima): Considered an allegorical rather than a historical figure, Vimalakirti was a layman of profound realization. The *Vimalakirti Sutra* tells of his use of illness as a skillful means to teach the Dharma: he became ill because "sentient beings are ill." In this sutra, sunyata is presented "as the joyous and compassionate commitment to living beings born from an unwavering confrontation with the inconceivable profundity of ultimate reality" (Robert A. F. Thurman, translator, *The Holy Teaching of Vimalakirti*). Vimalakirti appears in Case 84 of the *Blue Rock Collection*.

ZAZEN, J.: Literally, "sitting Zen" (also translated as "meditation"), the practice of sitting still in an alert posture (usually in some form of the lotus posture), in which the attention is at once one-pointed and diffuse, focused on the breath and aware of things just as they are.

ZENDO, J.: The hall or large room where zazen is practiced in a group. A small room in one's home may be dedicated as a zendo for daily practice.